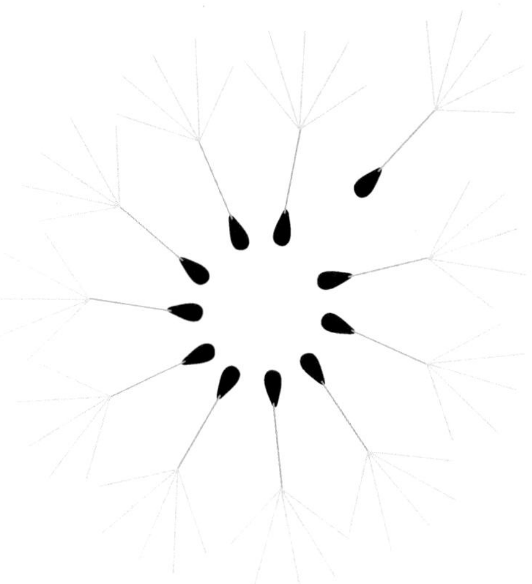

Here's what people are saying...

"This book is a treasure! In it you'll discover riches in wisdom, insight and perspective, as well as a map to get you started!"
—Derrick Sweet, Chairman of Healthy Wealthy and Wise Corporation and author of Get the Most Out of Life

"Insightful, thoughtful and creative. Celia brings great vision and direction to this work and applies her abilities to listen, reflect and guide with enthusiasm and openness. This book is Celia's gift to the world."
—Manal Aboelata, Program Director at the Prevention Institute

"Celia is nothing less than a master at her own craft. Her expert guidance allows her clients to step more fully into the empowerment and ownership of their lives. I highly recommend Celia's work to anyone who needs some clarity, insight, support and empowerment...in any area of their life."
—Delia Douglas Haight, CEO and Founder of DDH PR

"Within the first week of working with Celia, I booked a national spot, and the doors continue to fly open. Whether it's performing off-Broadway or finding happiness in the day to day, Celia's methods have taught me how to live a more fulfilling life. I highly recommend her work...but only if you want to live the life of your dreams."
– Jamie M. Fox, Actress, Producer and Writer

"Celia is a driven professional whose straightforward and customized approach provides her clients with the structure and focus they need to achieve their goals. As a master trainer, executive coach, public speaker, mother and wife, Celia understands the importance of having a successful work-life balance, and she leads by example."
—Tiana Sanchez, Life Coach at Designing Your Path

Published in 2012 by: Journey Publishing

Celia Ward-Wallace LLC

ISBN 978-0-578-09966-8

1. Self-Development
2. Spirituality

Cover Design: Elspeth Maxwell
Copy Editor: Morgan Stone
Printed and Bound in Los Angeles

For more information and to contact Celia Ward-Wallace directly for speaking engagements and events:
www.celiawardwallace.com, celia@celiawardwallace.com.

Dedication:

Joe, you are my one and only true love. I take you for eternity to be my lawfully wedded husband, to have and to hold from this day forward; for better or worse, for richer and for poorer, in sickness and health, in good times and in bad, until death do us part. We have been through all of that, and we are still going, stronger than ever! Thank you for loving my authentic self and always encouraging me to stand in my full power. Thank you for opening my eyes to a new perspective. Thank you for your positivity, creative genius and huge heart. You helped me to become whole again and inspired me to live my dream. Loving you was my first clear gift and I continue to follow my passion for you. You are my enchanted love and best friend forever. I love every moment of this journey with you and the girls by my side. Whatever may come, I know we will be just fine.

Foreword

When Celia Ward-Wallace asked me to write the foreword to her new book, *A Woman's Guide to Having It All: Life Lessons to Live By*, I was thrilled. Through the empowering Life Lessons, Celia reminds all women that they already have everything they need to live a life of contribution. Celia believes now is the time to focus on loving themselves, uniting with each other, following their dreams, being of service and connecting to their higher power. Each page provides wisdom and guidance to navigate the storms and challenges of life.

I know as well as anyone the importance of valuing and empowering women. I was born on the floor of an abandoned building with my twin brother. My biological mother put us up for adoption, and the most wonderful woman in my life, my mother Mamie Brown, adopted us, as well as five other children. She loved and cared for us all while working her fingers to the bone as a housekeeper for affluent families. She constantly strived to balance family life, work, finances and spirituality while building confidence and integrity in all of her children. She always encouraged me to follow my dreams, to have faith in myself, and to be of service to others. The lessons my mother taught me are the universal lessons of truth that Celia Ward-Wallace so passionately shares with you in this book.

I have given speeches all around the world, motivating people to live their dreams. Celia Ward-Wallace's voice is a gift to the world. She shares powerful success strategies she learned from the University of Hard Knocks. Each chapter is full of practical advice that will empower you to live your greatest life. Celia's passion and drive to make a difference in the world inspired her to write A Woman's Guide to Having It All to transform the lives of women and encourage them to manifest their greatness. This book will provide you the tools to carve out a life for yourself that will catapult you to new heights.

Celia is on a mission to mobilize a million women to stand in their power and live an achievement driven life. This book is a must-read for anyone who is ready to live the life they were created for. You have greatness in you and this book will help you share it with the world!

—Les Brown, Author of Live Your Dreams

CONTENTS

"There is only one journey. Going inside yourself."

-Rainer Maria Rilke

MY LESSONS LEARNED

My Journey From a Life Full of Fear to a Life Full of Faith, Purpose and Self-Love

I love being a woman. I am a huge fan of women, and I am rooting for us all to have the best lives possible. I come from a long line of dynamic and powerful women: My great-grandma Sarah was a Polish immigrant who toiled as a garment worker in the pogroms; my great-great-aunt Melinda was a public speaker on women's social issues of the time; my grandma Libby was a saleswoman and led a continuing-education program for seniors; and my grandma Melinda was a teacher and counselor for pregnant teens, as well as a patient advocate within the medical community. These women inspire me, as do all of you. I want to share my story with you in the hope that it will empower you and motivate you to live the life you were created to live.

My journey is about how I:

- Went from living a life full of fear to living a life with inner peace
- Went from being stuck in life to being unstuck and free in life
- Found my true calling and ability to share my gifts with the world
- Learned to have faith in myself and in my higher power
- Transformed from seeing the world as an individual, and focusing on my individual problems, to seeing the world with a unity consciousness, and that all living things are connected to each other

I hope that reading my story will motivate you to have faith in yourself, the universe and your dreams.

If you think about it, when conception occurs, there are millions of sperm racing to fertilize the egg. The one sperm that won the race combined with the egg to create you! When you were conceived, you had already won the biggest race of your life. Within that fertilized egg, you already had everything you needed to survive and thrive in this world. You came into the world a winner, whole and full of greatness. Sadly, people quickly begin the journey of defragmenting themselves and disconnecting with their greatness, worthiness and completeness. This explains why so many people are unhappy and are striving to fill the void inside by using outside measures of happiness—a large bank balance, a job with prestige, a luxury car. Little do they know that there is no amount of money, position in life or material thing that can heal their wounds and the pain they feel inside. Those issues are healed by love of self and others, love of work and service and a faith in a power greater than them; a faith that everything will be just fine.

Throughout my life I have learned many lessons, which I will share in the next part of this book. I will take you on a journey of my life and share the three main lessons that help me daily to live an authentic life: 1) I learned lessons about the search for safety and security; 2) I learned lessons about love and loss; and 3) I learned lessons about purpose, passion and faith. My hope is that you will see yourself in my story and use the tools in this book to help you have the abundance that is rightfully yours in this lifetime.

My Journey From Birth to Adulthood

My journey began when I was conceived. The choice to be born to my parents laid the foundation for everything I have become. I was born into a home with a lot of love but not a lot of money. My parents were well educated yet chose the working-class life of union organizers. Their choices to be organizers determined our income level. We were a low-income family, and over the years things improved, but in my early years, I felt the undercurrent of my parents' stress about money. My father was a union organizer at an automobile factory and suffered a back injury on the job. He went out on disability, had surgery and eventually got laid off. He used to say to me, "Celie"—my nickname—"come on in here and help your dad out." I remember being a little girl, and my tall, strong daddy couldn't reach down to tie his shoelaces. While he continued to organize a big campaign to keep his auto plant from closing, we were definitely living paycheck to paycheck. My mother, also a union organizer, was likewise laid off and decided to go back to graduate school.

For what my parents lacked financially, they made up for with love. We always had a roof over our heads, food in the refrigerator and attentive, loving parents. The normal child probably would not have noticed the financial strains, but from a very early age, I had the gift of being very attuned to other people. I was able to read their emotions, and I had the desire to help them. I remember when I was four my father worked the night shift at the auto plant. He would come home at 2:30 A.M., and I would always wake from sleeping to have a few minutes of undivided attention from him. We would talk about the day and all of the highlights and lowlights. My father always told me that I could see through him and read his emotions. If he came home in a bad mood, riddled with stress and fatigue, as much as he tried to conceal it from me, I could always tell. I would say, "Daddy, what's wrong? I know something is wrong." He would then share briefly whatever was bothering him and talk it through with me. I was sensitive to the financial stress and went out of my way to ease the burden on my family in any way I could, by helping out around the house and being a "good girl."

I internalized the responsibility to help my family, as if my small efforts would solve the problem. I became overly aware of money, and when my parents would buy my sister and me anything, I was always very modest, refusing multiple pairs of shoes or jackets, hoping that the savings on these items would help pay another necessary bill, as my father had done. I knew that money was tight, and I later learned that this experience formed a script in my subconscious mind that having a safe job with a good salary would provide safety, security and happiness.

As all great parents should, mine fostered in me self-reliance, confidence and love. In my household, the children were valuable members of the family, and our feelings, thoughts and opinions were welcomed and expected. We were a family unit—my mother, father, younger sister and I. My older sister, from my father's first marriage, and I were also very close. She lived with her mother in the California Bay Area, so we couldn't be together as much as we wanted. There was a lot of love, affection and play in my home.

My parents were political activists, intellectuals and atheists. They worked communally with other activists for common causes and had planning meetings several times a week. Everyone brought their kids along, and each night a lead organizer would rotate being in charge of the childcare. We would play games, watch movies and eventually fall asleep to the grumbling voices of our passionate parents in the adjacent room. At the ages of nineteen, nine and six, my older and younger sisters and I marched together in our first demonstration with picket signs, chanting *"Si, se puede"* with the masses of people fighting for their rights. I loved the feeling of community and the rainbow of people from different ethnicities and backgrounds. I understood the importance of fighting for your rights and for the underdog, so I was happy to be able to participate in furthering the cause.

My family ate dinner together every night. This made for lively meal conversations, and my parents encouraging my sister and me to develop our own beliefs and contribute to all of the conversations, even if it led to heated debates and arguments. At an early age, my gift of communication was evident, and my parents reinforced and fostered this gift. All the conversations I had with my parents were my training ground for reaching my calling of helping others find their power within.

Following the successful United Auto Workers campaign that, with broad community support, delayed the closure of the General Motors plant in Van Nuys, a community just north of Los Angeles, in 1989 my parents founded a non-profit civil rights organization called the Labor Community Strategy Center. Their organization fights for the rights of low-income people of color who have been ignored and neglected by society. The exposure to people in need and people dedicating their lives to service impacted my focus on social justice, humanity and community work very early. Although my parents were atheists, through their teaching and example, they instilled in my sister and me the values of kindness toward others, respect for all, self-determination, sharing of resources and working for the common good.

My parents strongly supported public schools, so I attended inner-city schools in Los Angeles. I was a natural leader, enjoying responsibility and wanting to unite people. In elementary school, I attended Carthay Center School, and I was the school vice president and a member of the leadership council. I was blessed to have a tight-knit circle of friends and their parents who represented many of the different ethnicities in Los Angeles. There were about ten boys and ten girls who were black, white, Latino, Asian and biracial, and they played together from kindergarten through the sixth grade. We were each other's best friends, boyfriends and girlfriends, and many of us are still connected to this day (thank you, Facebook!). My formative elementary years set the stage for my love of all people.

In junior high I attended John Burroughs Middle School, where I joined the track and basketball team, as well as the drama program. At this time the Gulf War was beginning, and having come from a long line of activists, I met with the school officials, announcing my intention to organize a school walkout against the war and violence as a form of resolution. It was not against the troops but against the initiative of taking the action to go to war. I spread the word among the students, and I also contacted media outlets. Days later a group of us formed the leadership committee and implemented our plan of action. We had a very successful walkout, and I was one of the main speakers against the war. We were covered by the media and made it onto CNN's television news coverage, seen globally.

I went on to high school at Fairfax Senior High, where I was the women's basketball team captain, as well as a part of the softball team. I loved team sports and the camaraderie and sisterhood it created. Sometimes I felt insecure inside, although I carried myself with confidence. Competing in sports and playing a leadership role helped me feel good about my body, feel accepted by other girls and feel proud of my accomplishments. At this time, there was rising tension between Latino and black youth at some of the local schools. In an effort to diffuse any such tension at my school and create mutual respect and tolerance, I created, with other students, a group called *Alliance*. This was a diverse group of students who met at lunch to discuss any issues or concerns they were having with other students, in addition to brainstorming efforts that we could implement at the school to create more understanding and cooperation among the students. I went classroom by classroom, spending five minutes pitching to the students to participate in *Alliance*, explaining that we could make a difference by celebrating our connectedness instead of our differences. The response was overwhelming, and our group made significant changes for the better within our school.

The combination of these influences and the room to be myself led me along my journey. My family was a very tight unit. My younger sister and I were attached at the hip, and I felt a very maternal bond to her. She was beautiful, funny and smart. She was the typical youngest child, who seemed to get away with more, have more outbursts and take up more space. I adored her and felt responsible for her. My parents instilled in us the importance of family, and we spent a lot of time together, going to the park and just hanging out, snuggling, watching a movie at home. Although my parents worked a lot, they always made our family a priority. They hosted every birthday barbecue bash until I was twenty-one, attended every basketball game, helped me write every research paper (including editing this book)—and my mother even made every one of my graduation and prom dresses. My family was everything to me, and the love I felt from them and for them was overwhelming. I developed a fear of dying and loss early on.

I was hyper-aware of all my blessings and how much my family meant to me. But instead of being fully present, enjoying them and relaxing, I would often be wracked with fear of losing them and what my life would be like without them. I loved them so much, and much of my identity was tied to my bond with my "family of origin." As I grew up, this manifested as my need to control many circumstances. I thought if I could stay one step ahead and think about everyone's needs, I was so powerful that I could prevent anything bad from ever happening.

Leading up to college, and throughout those four years, the need for security continued to manifest. My parents very generously paid my tuition and the majority of my expenses for college. My dad sat me down the summer before starting college and worked out a school budget for me. He showed me how much I was expected to contribute. It was time for me to start working, and the summer before college, at the age of sixteen, I got my first full-time job as a waitress. I worked all summer, and then through college I worked three jobs at a time. I attended UCLA and majored in World Arts & Cultures and Sociology. I specialized in inter-group conflict and prejudice, because I was fascinated by the dynamics between different groups and the ways in which we feel separated and united. I took many classes with my most influential professor, Jerome Rabow, where many of us stood in front of a class of two hundred and discussed our challenges with our race, class and gender identity. As a white woman raised in a predominantly black and Latino working-class community, I had plenty of issues to work through.

In addition to racial identity issues, I was often worried about money and would occasionally skip meals to try to save more. I wanted to have as much money in the bank as possible so I could always pay my bills and be protected in case of an emergency. I felt like having money in my bank account would make me feel secure and, therefore, happy, but that wasn't the case. Instead I was often controlling and anxious.

As a senior in college in 1997, I met Joe, my now husband of eight years, fourteen together. We began our long and transformative journey together. He was the opposite of me. I thought I was poor growing up, but he truly grew up in poverty. He was the only boy, with three sisters and a single mother. He tells a story of his mom buying a house that was going to be condemned, and the city giving Joe's mom twelve days to bring it to code. My husband was so handy; he went around to vacant abandoned homes, taking a toilet from here and a door from there, until the home passed inspection. He also was homeless for a period of time, living out of his car. He started a business painting address numbers on the curb for five dollars a home. He had faced truly trying times and knew that our position in life was so much better. He held the confidence that no matter what happened, we would be fine. He came to me with that profound understanding. Little did I know that, ten years later, I would be the one to remind him to have faith in ourselves and in a power greater than us.

Joe is a risk taker and believes that life is meant to be lived. He is gorgeous, charismatic, visionary and brilliant. We fell quickly and madly in love. We were so different from each other; from an outsider's perspective, they would have never put us together. He was black and I was white; he was a Christian and I was searching; he was divorced with three children, and I was never married, without any children. The differences between us never were an issue. Joe did and still does think I am the most beautiful woman he ever met. He always tells me, "If Halle Berry was to walk into the room right now, I wouldn't be able to take my eyes off of you." Fortunately, we have never had to put that to the test! He also understood who I was and has allowed me to always be myself and stand in my full power. We were crazy about each other and have always been and continue to be, inseparable.

Losing My Way and Becoming Stuck

When I graduated from college, I landed a safe, secure city job. I worked for the Recreation and Parks Department as a community center director. This continued to build my experience working in social services and connecting with different populations of people. I was growing and gaining wisdom to help me along my path. This job had a solid salary, great benefits and a great pension plan. It also allowed me to be involved in groundbreaking work, promoting equal access to sports for all girls and women. I was able to expose young women to the life-changing impact sports can have in their lives, just as it did in mine. In many ways it was rewarding, at least initially, but I couldn't express my full potential in that position, and I was settling. By all measures, I should have been happy, but like many people now, I was scared, stuck and living my life for external measures of security. Everything should have been great, but none of these things could quiet the fears of my inner child. I also was unconscious to the fact that the job was not stimulating for me, was not sufficiently challenging and was not the right fit. It took me more than ten years to figure that out! Thank God I finally did.

My parents were some of the original activists of the sixties era. They were in their early twenties when they joined organizations fighting for civil rights and women's empowerment. While many so-called hippies and activists of the sixties grew out of their activism, my parents continue to fight for those who have no voice. My parents' selflessness, commitment and sacrifice created large shoes to fill. I internalized their hard work as a script that unless I followed in their footsteps, no matter what I did professionally, it was not good enough. I knew that I wanted to serve others, but I judged myself harshly, thinking that I wasn't meeting their approval. It was a script that was formed from an early age.

I grew up on the front lines of so many social and political movements. I saw the entire behind-the-scenes theoretical and planning work my mother did, and I saw how much of a public leader and spokesperson my father was. My father tells a story of me going with him to make a speech to a bunch of college students about social movements and the need for activism. After the room of five hundred or so students gave him a standing ovation, I turned to him and said, "Dad, you are going to have so many people at your funeral." I saw how much my parents loved their work, and I wanted so badly to be like them, or to accomplish things on their level of impact. I internalized this pressure and thought that they would love me less if I didn't make the same professional choices they did. Even though this placed undue pressure and self-judgment on me, the positive side of their work's influence on me was my gaining an understanding that we should all give of ourselves to help others.

In my soul, I knew there was powerful work I was created to offer to the world, but I really didn't know what that was. I was good at many things, but nothing kept my interest and felt like the right fit. I thought maybe I was not going to be a career woman and, instead, since I had so many blessings in my life in the form of fabulous family and friends, that maybe that was where my focus and purpose would lie.

As I was searching for meaning, my husband suggested that although we both had "safe" jobs, we should simultaneously become entrepreneurs and get into buying income property. Joe had the foresight that it was the ideal time to get in, before the real estate craze, right in the beginning of it all. In 2001 we bought our first rental-income home for $72,000 in Palmdale, California. This was the beginning of our adventure in real estate and our contentious yet productive partnership. Over the years, the real estate transactions were very stressful and put a strain on our marriage, but we always pushed through stronger with an amazing outcome. We started with one rental property, and after ten years, we owned fifteen. By all measures, we were living large. We had access to lots of money, we had great credit, and we were in really good shape for our financial future and retirement. We vacationed multiple times a year, entertained frequently and were able to pay our bills with ease. However, this could not quiet my anxiety about money and my worries for the future. I had no faith in our resiliency, no faith in a higher power and no sense of purpose. Instead of giving me peace, these investments brought me more anxiety.

As time went on, I started to hear the voices in my head say, *You are supposed to go to graduate school. If you don't go now, you may never go, and you won't live up to your potential!* So I decided I should go to law school, since I'd heard the script from external influences from a very early age: "You will be a great lawyer someday." I knew I didn't want to be a lawyer, but I wanted to go to graduate school and thought the studies would be stimulating and would enrich me. I also thought it made sense at the time, since the field of law combined my gift of communication with my passion for helping people and fighting for social justice. I hadn't yet learned a very important lesson, which I now know: You should never do something because you are motivated by what others think you should do with your life; you should only move forward if the action will further something that you are already highly motivated to do.

Anyhow, I attended night school for four years at the People's College of Law, which is a small civil rights law school in Los Angeles. I was a standout student, but what I really excelled at was mentoring my fellow classmates. I would arrive early to class to teach review sessions, and I loved to hear about other students' life situations and to offer advice if prompted. I graduated and attained my Juris Doctorate degree. Around this time, I also conceived my first daughter. I sat for the bar exam and was so overcome with morning sickness that I spent almost as much time in the bathroom throwing up as I did taking the exam. I did not pass the bar in this first effort, within a very close margin. At the time I felt I had failed, and that I had wasted four years of my life. But I soon realized it was actually a gift in disguise, an obstacle created for me to learn from. I learned that I never really wanted to be a lawyer. I really loved being with people and helping them, but I preferred to do it in a more relationship-based setting. I also learned that I didn't want my job to be so time-consuming that I wouldn't have room for a balanced life. It was important to me to protect my time for my relationships and hobbies. So it really was a blessing that I didn't become a lawyer, because that would have taken me off course for some time. It could have taken years before I'd have gotten back on the right track, leading to my true purpose of empowering others through coaching, speaking and writing.

I always knew I wanted to be a mother—that was one thing I was never searching for. I knew it was a part of my journey. Having my two girls has been life altering. As all moms know, every cliché you ever heard about motherhood is completely true. *The love you have for your child is like no other love you've ever experienced. Being a mother is more work than you ever imagined, and it never ends. You will never sleep again; you put the needs of your children before your own and are lucky if you have anything left for yourself. Children remind you of the parts of yourself you never want to let die.* For me, motherhood calmed and settled me, as I knew I had found my place. It came naturally for me. I knew how to give love, time and affection freely, because my parents taught me how. I knew how to support my kids unconditionally, and how to listen to their thoughts and feelings without stifling them, because of the respect my parents gave me. Being a mom expanded the love in my heart for myself, and I became more confident about the love I had to give to others.

Facing Hardship and Failure

Around this time Joe became a firefighter. This was an exciting period because it appeared that this was another check off the list in an effort for security. While Joe had always been successful in his previous occupations, this one was different. He would now have a well-paying, secure job with great benefits. However, as if going through the fire academy was not hard enough, when he began his probation, we experienced our first encounter with racism as a couple. Joe is black and I am white, and when I began to visit him at his first fire station, he experienced harassment and discrimination from his superiors. They began to haze him and, on one occasion, made him complete a grueling drill over and over and over again, until his clavicle separated from his chest! This was a career-ending injury, although he was given a reasonably accommodating civilian position. We stood up for our rights, sued the fire department and received a winning settlement. However, this process took place over a period of five years, during which Joe faced depression, insomnia, feelings of inadequacy and physical pain. The man I knew and loved was lost for a long time; that period of time did its damage. He has since broken the shackles of these negative experiences and risen a stronger, wiser, more powerful man. Joe's case was one of many that changed the fire department's policies forever, to prevent any other person from being discriminated against and harassed the way he and others were.

Simultaneously, while we fought our case, Joe and I continued our mom-and-pop real estate operation, doing everything ourselves. A lesson we learned the hard way is that people are not gifted at everything. The areas in which you lack are ones in which you should rely on the expertise of others. This was never more apparent than in 2007, when the "real estate bubble" burst. We were not among the few who'd had the foresight to sell everything and protect their assets. We were pretty much blindsided. Over a period of time, we lost the bulk of our property and money, and this created more stress, worry and fear about the future. It also created a sense of loss, failure and all of the "If we only had..." and "What if?" tormenting thoughts, which we continued to ruminate. I had never struggled with depression, but I remember my thirtieth birthday in June 2007 being one of the saddest days of my life. This began a long period of sulking in pain and disbelief. I called all my so-called "advisers," and none of them had any advice that could take away the wrenching feeling in my stomach. I knew it was too late to do anything but brace myself for the steep fall that was coming.

On paper, this time of my life was the time of greatest failure. I was working at a job mainly for the security, and I felt stuck and unfulfilled. I lost most of my assets, my credit was damaged, and I had lots of debt. My husband lost his great job, was injured for life and lost his way. This was the moment when all of those fears from childhood became a reality. I realized my fear of losing security, I realized my fear of loss, and I realized my fear of failure. This was the closest to hitting rock bottom I have experienced in my lifetime. Our financial mini-empire crumbled over the course of three years. For a while, Joe and I lived in denial and disbelief. We were not quick to take action but, instead, avoided confronting our financial problems. We hoped our reality was somehow a bad dream, that we would wake up and our high-rolling life would reappear. That was not the case. Every day the unopened mail and the calls from bill collectors would haunt us. They were all reminders of falling short of our dream life.

Even though we needed to deal with reality and create a new plan, Joe and I were under so much stress that we avoided talking about things for fear it would create more conflict. The strain of all the challenges caused many arguments burdened with blame, defensiveness and miscommunication. We pointed the finger at each other and questioned the other's decisions. We retraced all the years, trying to understand where we went wrong and who was to blame. Did I hold us back with my need for safety? Did Joe make us vulnerable with his comfort with risk? Whatever it was and whoever's fault it was, we spent endless days feeling blue about it and being angry at each other. We were depressed, anxious and lost. For a long time, it was a struggle to get out of bed, and we only did so to keep a healthy home for our happy kids. In many ways, our kids were our saving grace. They woke up each morning with smiles on their faces, their hearts full of unconditional love, and they couldn't have cared less what kind of car we drove, or whether we traveled to Maui or stayed home. They wanted us to be present, to show them love and attention and to have fun. These are the simple things in life, which we too often forget about.

Our commitment to our marriage, our family and our faith was solidified during this time. We realized that our marriage and our children were really all we had left. We looked in the mirror and understood that our marriage had never been based on all of this "stuff" that we lost, but instead was based on love and devotion. Our relationship was truly tested, but it passed the test and became even stronger because of the challenges. These obstacles that tried to take us down—and did take down many marriages at this time—only fortified the strength of our relationship. We rallied together, faced our fears and handled our business. We no longer had all the money, but what we lost financially, we gained back and then some in gratitude, wisdom and faith in God.

Making the Shift to Wholeness

Instead of falling apart, I rose up. Like a phoenix rises from the ashes, so did I. I understood in that moment all that I had to be grateful for. I woke up, turned to my left and saw Joe lying there. I thought, *He's so handsome. I love him so much. Thank you for this man.* Then I thought, *Thank you for this warm blanket and this comfortable bed I am sleeping in. I heard a knock at the door, and my girls came running in. I thought, Thank you for these healthy, happy and loving children.* I realized in that moment that I had all the blessings I was searching for. It wasn't about the security of a job or a bank account; it was about love, gratitude and faith in myself and in a higher power. I realized money does not define you, and safety is just an illusion.

The combined hardship of the real estate crash and my husband's injury had a huge impact on our lives. We had every excuse to be sad, fearful and disappointed; however, this was the turning point I needed. These life-altering events were created by the rhythm of the universe to bring me into consciousness, so that I could evolve into the fullest expression of my highest self. These events brought meaning to me. All the fear I had about needing financial security and wanting things to be safe were turned upside down. I had faced my greatest fears and I was okay. In fact, I was more than okay; I was blessed. All my necessities were taken care of, and I was surrounded by love. The money and security were just things outside of me. They had nothing to do with me. At the end of the day, I looked around and found that I had blessings everywhere. I woke up each morning with air in my lungs, a beating heart and thoughts in my head. The love I shared with my husband grew stronger through all the hardship, and what could have easily divided us instead strengthened our commitment and our life story. Experiencing my greatest fears released them, along with all the worry and anxiety bottled up in them.

At this time, I started two different focuses. First, I began to study the greatest spiritual leaders of the past and of the moment. I narrowed it down to thought leaders who spoke to me, such as Dr. Wayne Dyer, Les Brown, Marianne Williamson, Oprah Winfrey, Deepak Chopra, Michael Bernard Beckwith, Iyanla Vanzant, Eckhart Tolle, Jon Kabat-Zinn, Mahatma Gandhi and Buddha. Growing up without religious or spiritual influences and guidance left me searching and longing for a sense of faith in something greater than myself. Through my study, I began to practice yoga, meditation, prayer and affirmations. I began to redirect my self-defeating thoughts and words and to focus on gratitude and a positive mental attitude. This was a time in my life when everything was falling apart around me on paper: My business was failing, my finances were in the toilet, and I was unfulfilled professionally. However, despite it all, I found peace. I faced all the demons that had once haunted me. The bottom fell out of the security I put in place to protect myself. When it did all fall apart, I looked around and saw that I was okay—that we were all okay. In fact, we were great. We had our health, we had one another, we had love and an abundance of blessings that could never compare to the wealth you find in your bank account. I had faced my fears and won.

At that time, I knew that, no matter what, everything would be fine. I would be able to face whatever hardships came my way and would overcome them a stronger and wiser person than before. I began to understand that life is all about the lessons. They are the way the universe teaches us in this lifetime. As Mao Tse-tung says, "Fall in pit, gain in wit." We all have to fail in order to get up stronger, and the next time we are faced with a similar obstacle, we will not make the same choices, because we learned the lesson the first time around. That is the goal, at least, because if you don't learn the lesson, it comes back around with bigger consequences for not being aware. I started to understand my role in the universe and that we are all connected to each other and everything else, like the earth, stars and planets. We are all created from love, and if we lead with love and faith in our beauty, then the world around us begins to mirror that perspective.

We are told to prepare for opportunities, and all of my life experiences prepared me for the opportunity to become enlightened about the true meaning of life. When the universe delivered it to me, I was a ready, willing and able servant. I now looked at life with purpose and passion, and my gifts began to flow through me at a dizzying speed. Instead of questioning what was happening, I embraced the journey, and the countless opportunities to love and be loved manifested. I monitored my actions and thoughts, and I stayed in the space of faith in self and a higher power, leading with love and peace toward others. This practice led me on the path to the fullest expression of my true self.

On and off for more than ten years, I attended counseling sessions and loved it. Therapy was like a classroom for me. I wanted to dive deeper into my own psyche to learn more about myself and unveil my deepest issues. Each week my therapist and I would discover new patterns of behavior, and I would have epiphanies, or "light bulb moments," as I like to call them. Then I would apply what I learned to my daily life, and I would grow, change and evolve into a new and improved version of myself. I loved the therapeutic process and became a certified community counselor through the Southern California Counseling Center. I took a six-month course that focused on the issues facing lower-income communities of color, with which I was so familiar from a lifetime of exposure through my parents' organization's work, my work with communities in recreation and parks, and my projects at the People's College of Law. We learned about poverty, gang violence, child molestation, domestic abuse and the underlying sociopolitical causes of the prevalence of these issues in poor communities. We learned how to understand these issues and to counsel people who are dealing with them. This course was transformative for me, to once again understand my privilege in the world and my duty to serve those in need. I was and will always be privileged as an educated white professional person.

These are benefits I hold that can never be taken away from me, that many others don't have working for them. For a period of time, I contemplated going back to school to become a psychologist, but my instinct swayed me away from this. I was still searching for purpose, and becoming a counselor was just another attempt to figure it out. It resonated with me, but again I knew it wasn't the right fit, and I didn't want to sacrifice the time away from my job and my family for something about which I was unsure.

Then I had another light bulb moment. I remembered my older sister once told me I should be a life coach, since I was the one everyone turned to for advice and for creating a plan for their lives. I looked into the field and decided to pursue becoming a life coach through the Certified Coaches Federation. I appreciated their philosophy that the most important qualities for being a great life coach are your own life experiences, be they personal, educational or professional. My trainer, who later became my business partner and mentor, Derrick Sweet, gave me the tools to combine with my life experience to help others change their lives. Becoming a life coach made sense in every ounce of my being. I wasn't trying to fit a mold or be something other than myself. I was using my God-given gifts to help others. This was it!

Over time, being a life coach has opened so many opportunities for me to help others. I use my gifts of communication and public speaking to conduct courses and seminars that motivate and empower people to love themselves, to be themselves and to find a platform to help others. I work with individuals, businesses, nonprofit organizations, women's groups and shelters to share my story and the life lessons that have changed my life. It was a long journey down many windy roads and dead ends, but when I found my place, there was no stopping me. Suddenly my life's journey made sense, and I was in the zone. The universe started and has never stopped sending me the opportunities to create the life of abundance and purpose I have always yearned for.

I have begun to create a new vision of financial security. I make a good income in my field, but the difference now is that I know no amount of money can bring me happiness. Happiness comes from within. When I began focusing on what matters most—love, faith, hope, oneness, service, gratitude and positivity—the doors of the world flew open to receive me and have not shut yet. Understanding how the scripts in my mind limited me and kept me stuck allowed me to embrace the power to redirect my thoughts, feelings and actions and to live my authentic life. Removing those blocks opened the window to allow me to step into the light and into my divine purpose.

My intention in writing this book is to share my story with you. I am every woman, and I have the same struggles, neuroses and fears. I battle with them daily and I win the battle, and so can you. This is because I am now aware of the guiding principles of life that the world is teaching us, which I will elaborate on in the next section of this book. I have awakened from, as Abraham Maslow outlines in the Four Stages of Competence, the "unconscious incompetence" coma I was in, living a life often based on what I thought I was supposed to do, motivated by the needs of others. Instead, I am now "consciously competent," flowing through life with a connection to everything and everyone around me. I am faithful in myself and in my higher power. I know how to quiet my mind, and my mind is at ease. I work every day to maintain this state with daily practice of meditation and prayer, as well as by guiding my thoughts, feelings and emotions so that they are aligned

with the life I was created to live.

My goal with this book is to inspire you to become unstuck in your life. You are divine just as you were created, and the only thing standing in the way of reaching all your dreams is yourself. Stop living in a daze and letting the daily grind of life have its way with you. Instead, get in the driver's seat of your life, and do the work to remove the negative influences and shift your way of seeing the world. Spend time doing the things you love, and surround yourself with people who only have your highest good in mind. You were created with greatness in you. It is your journey to learn the lessons that will help you reach your fullest and greatest expression of your highest self. My goal is for this book to be one of the stepping-stones on your journey and to remind you of the lessons the universe is teaching you. I want you to have the light bulb moment of realizing that the universe has already taught you this lesson, and this time you are going to learn it and understand it before the consequences of ignoring it become too great. Life is about love; lead with love for yourself, your family, your friends and your community. As you do so, the master plan for your life will unfold as the universe intended.

Congratulations! The fact that you are reading this means you are on your way to living the life for which you were destined! Every experience bears the fruit of an important lesson created just for you. When you open your eyes, mind and heart up to receive the lessons, you will claim your full power. You will begin the life you only dreamed of.

There are many lessons I have learned that I continue to remind myself of daily. This guide is full of all the lessons I have learned along my journey, which are universal life lessons from which all women can learn. This book is a guide for you to live

an authentic, purposeful and peaceful life. I want the best for you and only have your highest good in mind. As women, we don't have a lot of time to read a book, so keep this by your bedside or in your purse, and when you have five minutes, open it up, read one lesson and answer the questions at the end. Then take the next step in your journey with the enlightenment to live your best life and touch the lives of others. There are no limits on your life; whatever you can imagine, you can achieve. Set aside your fear, reject your limitations, and abandon your negative thinking. Instead embrace passion, embrace love and embrace faith. This minute is when it all begins!

"Heaven is where you'll be when you are okay right where you are."

-Sun Ra

Life Lessons to Live By

Love Yourself, You Are Perfect Exactly How You Are, You Are Worthy

Life Lesson #1:

When you were conceived, the uniting of the egg and sperm was your first and biggest accomplishment! The one sperm raced to the finish line and beat millions of other sperm to unite with the egg to come into existence. In that moment, you already had everything you needed to become a human being and thrive in this world. When we are born, unless we enter the universe through trauma, most of us come into the world whole and happy. It is all the experiences and influences we receive along the way that start to break us down, until we no longer remember what it is like to feel complete within ourselves, and we start the journey of trying to capture those early childhood feelings of complete self-worth and self-love.

Sarah Ban Breathnach reminds us in *Simple Abundance: A Daybook of Comfort and Joy:*

> "One of the surprises that comes when you catch glimpses of your authentic self is the discovery that she's such a positive, upbeat woman. She's always smiling. She's always calm. She's always reassuring. She exudes confidence. Who is this woman, you might ask, and does she bear

> any resemblance to you? Yes and no. This is who you are on the inside. The real you. If you don't act this way all the time, it's simply because you haven't evolved to a higher plane of existence yet."

When you start to cut yourself down or wallow in feelings of low self-esteem, remind yourself that you are worthy just because you were born, and that the special light of your being is perfect just the way it was created. There is now and will ever be only one you in the eternal universe. You are magnificent. You are worthy. As Miguel Ruiz reminds us in *The Four Agreements,* "You don't need the acceptance of others. You don't need knowledge or great philosophical concepts. You have the right to be you, and express your own divinity by being alive and by loving yourself and others."

Questions:

1. What do you love about yourself mentally, physically and spiritually?

2. What lessons would you teach your children about self-love and confidence that you should apply to yourself?

"Learn the craft of knowing how to open your heart and to turn on your creativity. There's a light inside of you."

-Judith Jamison

You Have a Natural Calling and Unique Gifts to Share With the World

Life Lesson #2:

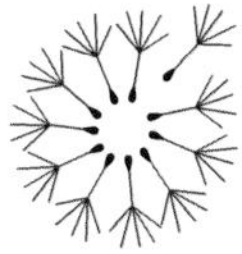

Each of us enters the universe with specific gifts to share. The various influences we receive throughout life often derail us into work that is "safe" and "smart," but often it is not work that is fulfilling or purposeful. We learn from our parents, teachers, religious leaders, politicians and media at a very early age many messages, such as: *Education is the key to success; it is important to have a good job that is secure; it is better to play it safe than to take risks.* All of these messages become ingrained in our subconscious mind at such a deep level that we accept them to be our own beliefs. We also experience parents, teachers, friends and religious leaders who either unintentionally or intentionally degrade us and undermine our self-esteem by not recognizing our gifts, not fostering our gifts or outright breaking down our confidence to such a level that we believe we have no gifts. The outcome of these experiences generally leads people down a painful and unhappy path toward an invisible life full of unconscious decisions with unpleasant outcomes.

We each are created with a calling and purpose to deliver to the world. We are meant to have a life full of purpose and passion. Dig deep to examine what excites you and what tools, skills and interests you have to share with others. Reject the negative voices you hear, which will attempt to limit your life, and instead embrace the world of possibility and creativity to dream of the life you want. Trust your inner voice and experiment with exploring these buried interests. Your gifts can lead to a hobby or an avocation, to community service or to a part-time or full-time career. It is not about how much time you spend doing these things; instead the importance comes from recognizing what your talents are and what you love doing. Once you accomplish that, you can explore in which capacity these skills and experiences can be introduced into your life, and you can begin the journey of embracing your worthiness and perfection.

What a relief to finally find your place, to find your calling! Some of us are born with the clarity, and others of us, like myself, search for a long time, knowing we are destined for a greater purpose but not knowing what that purpose is. In *Discovering Your Purpose,* Ivy Haley concurs:

> "Each of us is endowed with specific talents and abilities that are programmed into our being. These attributes aren't acquired: They're natural to us, 'written in' before we're born. You can take a step toward determining your purpose by discovering your unique talents and skills, especially those that cause you joy when you use them."

I always suggest that we embrace the self-discovery journey and think about all of the things in our life that spark interest in us and hold our attention. Make a list of all the things you love to do or would love to do. Then slowly and methodically make your way through the list, exposing yourself to different interests; see how they make you feel and if you want to continue to explore more deeply. For me, I have always been a jack-of-all-trades, master of none. I generally excelled at almost everything, but I was never great at anything that I could identify, and no particular discipline really spoke to me. So I made a list of all my potential interests: gardening, interior design, cooking, sports, counseling, dancing and more. Then I began categorizing them based on things I thought interested me as a hobby and things I thought were potential career options. Mind you, all the while, I was working a full-time job that I was good at and enjoyed, but which was not my calling. I knew there was something more for me. I took the things that I identified as hobbies, such as dancing and cooking, and when I had a little free time, I would do an activity in that area. I went out dancing with my girlfriends more frequently, and I started searching for recipes that were easy and healthy and that everyone loved. These were small efforts I made to listen to my inner voice saying these areas called to me and to explore them deeper. Spending time doing these things enriched my life, and I enjoyed them very much, but they did not fill the void of my true divine purpose, so I checked them off the list.

For the categories I identified as potential career options, I took one at a time and researched small ways that I could take an adventure in exploring them. So for gardening, I created and implemented the landscape design for my home. This was an attempt to see the process of a landscape artist, and whether I enjoyed the experience enough to take a deeper step to explore it as my true calling. I loved the experience, but that was as far as I decided to go in that field.

Another example was taking a certification course in community counseling. This journey confirmed to me that I was on the right track, because I loved the experience and was charged up by making authentic connections with people, discussing social issues and strategizing solutions. Ultimately, this process of exploring all potential areas of interest led me to the life coaching and professional speaking field, which ended up being exactly where I was supposed to be all along. I realized my whole life of education, professional experience and life lessons had always been leading me there. I finally found my calling and purpose, and it fit so well, there was no denying it. How did I know it was my calling? I knew because, by being myself and by using the gifts I was created with, I was able to connect with so many people and help them. I did not have to overthink things or push the work forward, and there was never any stress involved. I loved the work and was happy to spend my days doing it. Being a life coach and speaker was the right fit for me because I used my strengths of communication, planning, vision, creativity, mentorship and entrepreneurial knowledge.

Each of us wants to be able to do work that uses our gifts, and for the universe to mirror back to us the confidence that we are exactly where we are supposed to be. This journey is about unfolding that gift in order to share with the world the best version of ourself. In *The Power of the Subconscious Mind*, Joseph Murphy states that:

> "The happiest man is he who constantly brings forth and practices what is best in him. Happiness and virtue complement each other. The best are not only the happiest, but the happiest are usually the best in the art of living life successfully. God is the highest and best in you. Express more of God's love, light, truth and beauty, and you will become one of the happiest persons in

the world today."

We must rise to the occasion to be our best self and to give back to the world the best of us. We must not push along our journey with urgency to get to the next step, but instead embrace it and be present at this step, and be our most conscious and enlightened self.

Questions:

1. If money wasn't a concern, what would you spend all day doing?

____

____

____

____

____

____

2. What talents and gifts do you have that you haven't yet explored?

____

____

____

____

____

____

3. What actions/steps will you take to move forward in exploring these gifts?

____

____

____

____

____

____

"Many women today feel a sadness we cannot name. Though we accomplish much of what we set out to do, we sense that something is missing in our lives and - fruitlessly - search "out there" for the answers. What's often wrong is that we are disconnected from an authentic sense of self."

-Emily Hancock

Be Yourself, Live an Authentic Life

Life Lesson #3:

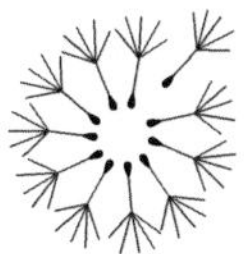

One of the steps in learning to love yourself is understanding just how special and unique you are. There is only one you. In the eternal universe, there has never been and will never be another being that has your individual soul. You were created with greatness instilled in you for a plan of greatness in life. The only thing limiting reaching those depths of self-love and outward love toward the world is you! As Les Brown shares in *It's Not Over Until You Win!,* "It is not only within your power, it is your absolute right to experience and enjoy the best that life has to offer."

Being a woman in modern society is challenging with all the social pressure and expectations on us to knock it out of the park in all aspects of our life. Society socializes us with programs to believe we are supposed to be highly educated, highly paid as a professional, be a "Stepford" wife, a devoted and always available mother, a housekeeper, cook, financial manager, sex expert, healthy and in great shape—and all with a gentle, obedient and happy attitude. Clearly this is an impossible standard to achieve. It is one thing to be motivated toward any of these goals from within; it is another to contort ourselves into a pretzel trying to be what we think everyone around us wants us to be. We think we are helping others and being selfless when, in reality, we are short-changing all of those around us. We are certainly able to accomplish a lot, run our homes and work like machines, but we are often resentful and angry, and we take it out on those around us and ourselves. Then we beat ourselves down some more, ashamed of our behavior, feeling like failures, unable to be perfect in all situations. The reality is that this occurs because our actions are not coming from a place of authenticity. Marxism teaches that women's work in the home and with the family is "invisible labor" that isn't paid for and allows greater profit.

Sarah Ban Breathnach points out in *Simple Abundance: A Daybook of Comfort and Joy*,

> "As you learn to acknowledge, accept and appreciate what it is that makes you different [...] the process begins. As you learn to trust the wisdom of your heart and make creative choices based on what you know is right for you, process becomes progress. As you learn to endow even the smallest moment of each day with Love, progress becomes reality perfected. [...] You become not only real to those who know and love you, but Real to everyone. You become authentic."

When you make the shift toward being authentic, you practice self-love and communicate with those around you about your abilities and limitations. This relieves the self-imposed pressure to be perfect and frees you up to take on what you can handle. Then you can practice patience toward those you love and allow some things to fall by the wayside.

Questions:

1. What qualities do you have that you love about yourself?

2. What qualities would you like to develop?

"The journey of a thousand miles begins with one step."

-Lao Tzu

Embrace Your Journey, and Have Faith That Everything Will Be Fine

Life Lesson #4:

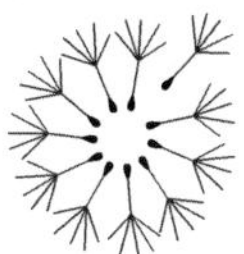

It is liberating to let go of control. It is really hard for women, in particular, to do so. We have spent so much of our lives and our loved ones' lives planning every detail of the day that we think it brings us comfort to do so—that somehow, by planning the details, we can control the outcome. But we really can't, and then when things don't go as planned, we are not flexible or patient, and everyone around us suffers. As much as we want to, we can't control what happens in our lives; we can only control ourselves.

So many of us live in fear of what will happen next. It prevents us from being present in the moment and allowing authentic connections. In *The Power of Now*, Eckhart Tolle explains fear.

> "The psychological condition of fear is divorced from any concrete and true immediate danger. It comes in many forms: unease, worry, anxiety, nervousness, tension, dread, phobia and so on. This kind of psychological fear is always of something that *might* happen, not of something that

> is happening now. You are in the here and now, while your mind is in the future. This creates an anxiety gap."

If we concentrate on channeling our thoughts to focus on the positive and channeling our actions to come from a place of kindness and love, then we have done our part. The rest we need to let go to the universe and embrace the journey. We don't know what tomorrow will bring, but if you know that you will be fine regardless of what may come, it releases the pressure of not knowing. You are free to let it all go and instead have faith that you are smart, skilled and capable, and no matter what the outcome, you will always be fine and will always land on your feet. Everything will be fine, no matter what. Have faith in your resiliency and ability to overcome anything and to be stronger and better because of it. As Les Brown encourages us in *It's Not Over Until You Win!*, "No matter how difficult your life may become, no matter how hard it gets, there is always reason to keep on going and fighting, because you can survive and thrive."

Questions:

1. What fears are controlling your life?

____
____
____
____
____
____

2. How does trying to control everything impact those around you?

____
____
____
____
____
____

"There is enough in the world for everyone to have plenty to live on happily at peace and still get along with their neighbors."

-Harry S. Truman

Be the Peace You Want to See in the World and in Others

Life Lesson #5:

If you ask most people what changes they want to see in the world, many would respond with "world peace." If you ask most people what changes they want to see in themselves, many would say they want "inner peace." Peace is contagious. It works on the principle of "paying it forward." If this book reaches only one woman who begins to embody peace in her life, I know she will transform others, and the snowball effect will begin. Inner peace comes from an awareness of your thoughts, emotions and actions. When you are thinking negatively about yourself and others, it is hard to have inner peace. When you have negative thoughts, this creates emotions of pain, suffering, anger, depression, anxiety, worry and fear. These emotions are the opposite of inner peace. When you have negative thoughts and feel terrible, you act out to those around you. These actions draw negative energy back to you, and this cycle is introduced into the world. The same is true for a cycle of positivity and peace. When you recognize yourself thinking negatively, you can be aware and monitor the thoughts. You can say, "I see that I am thinking negatively, and I choose not to think this way, so I am going to replace those thoughts with positive ones." You can then replace the thoughts with an affirmation or a factual reason that the thought is untrue. The more you practice this process, the less negative thoughts will appear.

Also, when you are feeling negative emotions, you need to be aware of them. Don't bottle them up. You need to release them in a healthy way. You need to get rigorous exercise, meditate, practice deep breathing, see a counselor, work with a life coach or call a friend. Don't ignore your feelings, because they manifest in the unkind ways you treat yourself and others. When we are acting badly toward ourselves or others, again we must be aware of it and stop ourselves in our tracks. The only way to change behavior is to recognize it. Dr. Wayne Dyer reminds us in *The Power of Intention*,

> "Remember that your natural state is joy. You are a product of joy and love; it's natural for you to experience these feelings. You've come to believe that feeling bad, anxious or even depressed is natural. Remind yourself as frequently as necessary: I come from peace and joy. I must stay in harmony with that which I came in order to fulfill my dreams and desires."

Once you have increased your awareness of your thoughts, feelings and actions, you can stay in constant connection with yourself, monitoring what is going on for you. When you start to fall into negative traps, use the tools you know to pull yourself out. When you wake up in the morning, say an affirmation: "Today I will be the peace I want to see in the world and in others." The more you focus your energy on love, kindness and peace, the more opportunities to reinforce these efforts will gravitate toward you. You will begin to overflow with the kindness coming your way and the open heart you have toward yourself and others.

Questions:

1. What negative thoughts and statements do you think about yourself and others?

2. What positive affirmation statements can you replace these with?

"Today a new sun rises for me; everything lives, everything is animated, everything seems to speak to me of my passion, everything invites me to cherish it."

-Anne De Lenclos

See Beauty Everywhere

Life Lesson #6:

It doesn't take much to see beauty all around ourselves. There is beauty in your children's faces, in your home, in the trees that line the street, in the smile of your coworker, in the body and mind that is with you at all times. The problem is that many of us are living our lives in an unconscious state. We have fallen into a hypnotic state of being, where we go through each day barely trying to make it to the next moment. We feel like our lives are constantly going, the demands on us are overwhelming and we have no control over our lives. We need to understand that this state of living in a brainwashed, unfulfilled state of mind is not natural. We were not created to chase success and accumulate things. We were created as the most advanced and beautiful beings. The human body is a great thing to focus on in order to become more conscious. It reminds us of how powerful, complex and beautiful we are. Jon Kabat-Zinn reiterates in, *Wherever You Go, There You Are: Mindfulness Meditation in Everyday Life*, "Perhaps the most 'spiritual' thing any of us can do is simply to look through our own eyes, see with eyes of wholeness, and act with integrity and kindness." When we choose to look for beauty in our life wherever we turn, the clouds start to lift, and we begin to feel fulfilled by all of life's greatness instead of weighed down by life's pressures to live an existence based on someone else's standards.

Who is the happier woman: the one who has a high-profile job, making a ton of money doing something she doesn't love, sacrificing her time with family and friends and self-care; or the one who has a lower-paying job in a field she loves, who lives a simpler life with less material things, who has time for family, friends, exercise and hobbies, as well as more free mental space? To me, the second woman is on the right track, is lucky to have learned the lessons of life earlier than others and will probably not suffer as much. She values life and beauty in all things and stops to smell the roses, literally observing the miracle of nature and the creation of all things.

If you shift your mindset to start looking for the beauty all around you, your heart will be flooded with the love you feel. As Derrick Sweet encourages in *You Don't Have to Die to Go to Heaven,*

> "You may notice a shift in your consciousness. You may start to see yourself in others without even trying. Later you may begin to see all of humanity in others. Before long, you may even begin to find God in everything—in a bird's song in the morning, a baby's cry, the sound of the wind and even in a dog's bark. I don't know why it happens, but it does. And it is heaven."

It is easy to do because beauty is all around you, starting with yourself. When you learn to love yourself, you open yourself up to all of the love surrounding you.

Questions:

1. Where do you see beauty in your life?

2. What shifts can you make in your life to see more beauty?

"Nothing ever strikes without warning."

-Danny Glover

Recognize and Learn From the Teachers and Lessons Designed Just for You

Life Lesson #7:

Have you ever wondered about the purpose of your journey of life? Well, if you really look at it, you will recognize that each day you encounter people and experiences that are teachers and lessons from which you can learn and grow. When we are met with a stressful event, it is common to for us to say, "Why me? Why is this happening to me?" It is useful to examine the reasons it is happening. Although many argue that much of life is unexplainable, we can also say that there is a lesson in everything. We can gain so much from opening ourselves up to these "teachers" when they present themselves each day. We can make eye contact with the people in the elevator, or say, "Hello, how is your day going?" to the cashier when we buy our coffee. You will be amazed to see, first, how surprised people are that you are actually taking an interest in them. Secondly, you never know the kind of conversation you will have. Often you are able to impart some knowledge that truly helps the other person, or they are able to share with you something that enlightens you as well. Finally, you are connecting to others, which is our natural purpose, to find the unity in all of us. As a result, you can reflect on your interaction and find ways to grow from it.

To become our best selves, we need to open ourselves

up to the world and all of the people in it. By being aware of the experiences we have, we can use them as a way to examine the implications for our own lives. As Eckhart Tolle, in *A New Earth*, states, "Life will give you whatever experience is most helpful for the evolution of your consciousness. How do you know this is the experience you need? Because this is the experience you are having at this moment." For example, when I go to the doctor, they give apples to the patients. I always take a few extras, knowing that there will be someone in need of food nearby. Then, as I drive to a stoplight and see a homeless man with a "Food" sign, I know I have an apple to share with him. I give the homeless man the apple, look into his eyes to show respect and connection, and know this could be me at any time. I am immediately flooded with emotion. This is a teaching moment for me. Instead of being disconnected from myself, I am aware and probe deeper. What just happened? Why was I so touched? Upon deeper examination, I realize I felt the emotion for many reasons. The emotion possibly came from: my connection with the man and realizing his struggle; feelings of appreciation and gratitude that I do not have to struggle in my life like the homeless man; and my own desire to help more people through increased service work. These are all important realizations from being open to the teachers and lessons in our lives that can be extremely useful.

Questions:

1. What lessons has the universe taught you lately?

____

____

____

____

____

____

2. How can you be more open to connecting with others?

____

____

____

____

____

____

"The ego needs recognition. The spirit does not need to thank itself."

-Stuart Wilde

There Are Two Parts of You: Your Higher (True) Self & Lower (False) Self -You Are Not Your Ego

Life Lesson #8:

This principle is complex and powerful, and once understood, it is truly life transforming. In our mind there is our ego (false self) and our true self. The ego is the part of our brain that actively tries to keep things at status quo. It is the part that lives in safety mode, protecting our scared inner child with thoughts and actions manifested around attachment to material things, feelings of scarcity and judgment of ourself and others. Our true self is felt when we are in a conscious state, experiencing the moment and all the beauty around us. This occurs when we shut off the constant voice in our head, release the labels on everything and everyone, and just be in the true essence with which we were created. In *A New Earth*, Eckhart Tolle explains what happens once we become aware of the separation between the ego and our true self.

> "You then no longer derive your identity, your sense of who you are, from the incessant stream of thinking that, in the old consciousness, you take to be yourself. What a liberation to realize that the 'voice in my head' is not who I am. Who am I

> then? The one who sees that. The awareness prior to thought, the space in which the thought—or emotion, or sense perception—happens."

Becoming conscious of the ego and nurturing our true self is a constant battle, which becomes easier as we strengthen our consciousness muscle. The more we recognize the negative impact of the ego and put it in its place, the easier it becomes to let the complexity of our greatness shine through. We need to work daily to overcome the attempts to sabotage our authenticity by our ego. Sarah Ban Breathnach explains in *Simple Abundance: A Daybook of Comfort and Joy,*

> "The ego has everything to lose once your authentic self grows strong enough to act consciously on your behalf, guiding your creative choices, decisions, ambitions and actions for your highest good. What was standard operating procedure before—denial, sublimation, repression—is recognized for what it is: subtle self-abuse. When you become authentic, you become greater than you ever thought you could be, and this greatness allows you to heal yourself, your family and your world. Your authentic self is your ego's worst nightmare, and the ego will do everything in its power to eliminate her rival's influence from your daily round. The way the ego goes about this is to bring in the heavy guns: fear and intimidation."

Well, let it bring in the heavy guns. Now that we are aware of the role the ego plays in holding down our true selves, we can defeat it, overcome the obstacles and embrace our metamorphosis into the highest expression of our true self.

Questions:

1. What limiting messages does your ego tell you to prevent your true self from shining through?

____
____
____
____
____
____

2. What will you feel when you step into the greatness of your authentic self?

____
____
____
____
____
____

"Gratitude unlocks the fullness of life. It turns what we have in to enough, and more. It turns denial into acceptance, chaos to order, confusion to clarity. It can turn a meal into a feast, a house into a home, a stranger into a friend. Gratitude makes sense of our past, brings peace for today, and creates vision for tomorrow."

-Melody Beattie

Remember That Gratitude and Service Give Our Lives Meaning

Life Lesson #9:

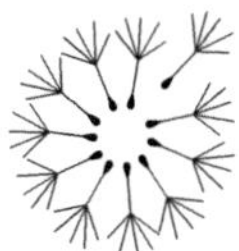

Every day that we wake up, we have a reason to be grateful. Then, if we look a little further, we all find many more things for which we can be grateful. Whether it is our partner lying next to us, or the warm blanket covering us, or the roof over our head, or the sunlight shining in, there is much to be grateful for. Granted, throughout the world, people live in various conditions of hardship; some are very poor and without basic necessities, and others have financial comfort with a life of privilege and many material goods. However, regardless of our financial standing, we are all unified by our commonalities of being living human beings who have been granted this moment in time to live our lives. In itself, this is a very important thing to be grateful for, and beginning to actively recognize it can be very motivating. Dr. Wayne Dyer reminds us in *The Power of Intention*,

> "Be grateful for those whose presence may have caused you pain and suffering. Be thankful to your Source for sending them, and to yourself for attracting them. They all had something to teach you. Now be grateful for everyone God sends to your path, and know as a co-creator that it's up

to you to either resonate with the high, loving energy of intention and keep those like-energized people in your life, or give them a silent blessing and a pleasant 'no, thank you.'"

When we start to look at our life from a place of gratitude, we find happiness and peace in the smallest gestures and interactions that happen throughout our day. These positive experiences are exponentially greater when we focus on the importance of service to our community. This can be volunteering at our child's school, donating old clothes to charitable organizations, teaching educational workshops, helping take care of our children and elders and guiding someone along the path of their purpose. As Marianne Williamson reminds us, "In every community, there is work to be done. In every nation, there are wounds to heal. In every heart, there is the power to do it." Regardless of the form, giving back to others and our world creates harmony, flow and positivity, and this all leads to many more things about which all of us can be grateful.

Gratitude is a guiding principle to use when creating our life's goals and dreams. We may create a plan for the next six to twelve months and want to attain certain things during that period of time. However, we will not be able to enjoy those accomplishments if we don't pay attention, on a regular basis, to all that we already have to be thankful for, and if we don't keep in mind to not take those things for granted. If we stay on track with a gratitude mind-set, then we will be that much more empowered by the success we achieve, because we will feel it with greater significance. Additionally, by guiding ourselves to focus a portion of our day or week on creating acts of service, whether small or large, we will have a greater connection to the world around us and become part of the healing force needed in the world. We will rise to our role as leaders and active participants in society as a whole. This is motivating, empowering, meaningful and sorely needed.

Questions:

1. What are ten blessings that you have to be grateful for today?

____

____

____

____

____

____

2. What makes these blessings special?

____

____

____

____

____

____

"We must learn to love everyone,
everything, everywhere."

-John Randolph Price

We Are All Connected and One

Life Lesson #10:

One of the major sicknesses our society battles with is individualism. Where did we get the idea that we are supposed to focus on ourselves and take care of ourselves without caring for the needs and lives of others? We are raised to think about the American Dream of having a house, a car, a job and freedom. In reality, this is only attained by the few; most others struggle in one way or another. Is it possible that there is such a disparity and so many struggles because we don't see ourselves in others?

We are all made up of energy. I am energy and so are you, and we were both created from the same source of energy. We are beings created to be interdependent and to live communally. Every fiber of our being is made to be connected to each other. However, for many this concept is very foreign. Many feel a disconnection from others and the world at large. They are struggling, and they can only think about the next moment and how they will get through the day. I get that. What I am saying is that by becoming aware of our natural connection to each other, we open up our eyes to the unity between us all. When you start making eye contact with people on the bus, or talking to the waitress, or saying hello to the elderly man on the street, you instantly feel a sense of warmth, of love, of oneness. We have all experienced being flooded with emotion when we've pushed ourselves to make a kind gesture toward a stranger. That feeling is not happenstance; it is the universe telling you that you are on the right track. Keep going...the more you connect with others, the more your heart will heal, the more their heart will heal, and the love will spread. Each person can cause a chain reaction of paying forward the love by recognizing the oneness of us all. One woman's suffering is your suffering. That could be you in a blink of an eye, and how important would it be for someone to shine kindness on you and pay attention to you?

We all want to be loved, we all want to have peace, we all want to be happy—these are things we all share. There is so much more that we all share than there are differences that divide us. We would never pay attention to the differences in the first place if it weren't for the social programming we receive every day of our lives. We are not the scripts in our head; we are beautiful, loving spirits that were created to love others and share our gifts through service. Derrick Sweet recommends in *You Don't Have to Die to Go to Heaven,*

> "Choose an hour, one day. For that hour, every time you encounter other human beings, look into their eyes and try to see an extension of you in them, and vice versa. [...]Our society promotes the illusion that we are separate from everyone, so this kind of openness could feel dangerous. Your ego may feel very threatened; this is quite normal, since we have been misguided for so long. Don't give up."

You are not ever alone. Just look around and you will see yourself in another right next to you. Reach out to others seeing the oneness in you, and you will be lifted in light to the highest expression of yourself. Your life will start moving forward in a positive way, becoming aligned with the life you were created to live.

Questions:

1. In what ways can you connect more with others?

____
____
____
____
____
____

2. How can you and your loved ones share your resources?

____
____
____
____
____
____

"Infinite riches are all around you if you will open your mental eyes and behold the treasure house of infinity within you. There is a gold mine within you from which you can extract everything you need to live gloriously, joyously, and abundantly."

-Joseph Murphy

Approach Your Life Believing in Unlimited Possibility and Creativity

Life Lesson #11:

When we are born, although some of us experience trauma, most of us enter into the world with a belief that the world is a happy place filled with happy people. Our souls tell us that we too will live a life of joy, and that we can achieve anything our minds and hearts can imagine. In modern society, this moment of wholeness is brief, a tiny window of possibility before outside influences begin to break down these positive and creative, natural ways of being. We become influenced by everyone and everything that surrounds us, and our beautiful child mind begins the process of becoming programmed. This occurs simply by our parents telling us, "In order to be successful in life, you must get a secure job," or our pastor telling us, "People who do not have the same faith as us are different," or the local news station filling our minds with images of violence and poverty. The once whole, open and creative soul of our being often turns into the fearful, anxious and unhappy mind of a woman stuck in her undesirable life situation, not knowing there is any way out.

To overcome being stuck, reconnect to the original essence of your soul as first created. Search for your higher self, who has dreams for your life and feels that the world is full of possibility. This involves removing the layers of programming we received from the world and brainstorming what natural passions lie beneath the layers. This can be achieved by reflecting on an earlier time of lightness and creativity, thinking about what we enjoyed doing, what we wanted to be and how we envisioned our lives unfolding before the weight of external influence. Barbara Sher writes in *Wishcraft: How to Get What You Really Want,*

> "There is nothing in this world that's worth doing that isn't going to scare you. The moment you make the commitment to going for your dreams, you begin to venture into the unknown. And the human organism's natural response to novelty and risk is adrenaline. Butterflies in the stomach. Wobbly knees. Pounding heart. [...]Comfort is one of the things you can forget about right now. You're not going to have it anymore. Excitement, company, help and support, yes. Comfort, no."

So, remove the "I should" and the "I have to," and think outside of the box. There is no risk in putting fears aside long enough to try to uncover one's true essence and guiding light. As Les Brown pushes us to understand in *Live your Dreams,*

> "With a powerful hunger for your dreams driving you, you will be surprised at the ideas that will come, and the people you will be able to attract, and the opportunities that will unfold. You will be able to see things that you won't be able to believe you didn't see before—things that may have been there right in front of you the whole time."

Questions:

1. What dreams do you have for your life that you haven't realized yet?

____
____
____
____
____
____

2. Imagine you have achieved these goals. What does it look like? What do you feel? And what do you hear yourself saying?

____
____
____
____
____
____

3. What activities can you participate in that will foster your creativity?

____
____
____
____
____
____

"There are two things over which you have complete dominion, authority and control - your mind and your mouth."

-Molefi Assante

Align Your Conscious and Subconscious Minds to Reach Your Goals

Life Lesson #12:

Most of us have not studied the brain and the relationship between the conscious and subconscious minds. For me, once I started to understand the relationship between the two and the actions I could take to align them, my life began to flow in the direction I wanted it to go. Your conscious mind is the part of the mind that has the thoughts, speaks the words and sets the intentions about what you want in your life. So, for example, you may use the will power and determination of your conscious mind to say, "This year I intend to meet the man of my dreams and, a year from now, be in a committed and loving relationship." Then you may realize months later that, although your intention was to find a significant other, you have not made any strides forward toward that goal. This can be de-motivating and discouraging. What many of us don't understand is that setting the intention in our conscious mind is not good enough, and this goal will not be actualized as long as the subconscious mind is not aligned with this goal. In this way, the subconscious mind undermines the intention with the old-sediment programming.

The subconscious mind is the part of your brain that is constantly at work, and you don't even notice it. It is the part of your brain that holds the memories of your life and incorporates all the programming you receive throughout your life from your family, teachers, religious figures, television, magazines and all images, words and thoughts to which you have ever been exposed. From an early age, we are all influenced by everything around us, good and bad. We take it all in, and our subconscious mind believes it all to be true and sets the wheels in motion to try to reinforce this programming. Although your goal may be to find a great man and have a loving relationship, if in your subconscious brain you have programming that says, "I will never be loved," "No man will ever want to marry me" or "I am not worthy of a healthy relationship," is it any wonder that you wouldn't meet the man of your dreams?

The process of aligning your conscious and subconscious is so important and effective, because once you begin to notice all the programming and negative thoughts, you can begin the process of replacing it with positive and loving thoughts and influences. When you notice the words people around you are saying, the violent or negative TV shows and movies you are watching, and the self-defeating talk you use, you can monitor these influences and change them for the better.

As far as the images, you have complete control over these; all it takes is awareness. If you spend your time reading celebrity tabloid magazines and watching crime shows, mainstream news or action movies, it is no surprise that your mind will be filled with programs of inadequacy, fear, anxiety, worry and disorientation. Remember, your subconscious mind seeks out evidence to prove your thoughts to be true. So the more you fill your brain with all of this junk, the more junk you will draw into your life. How will you ever find your true self and wonderful life under all of that? The answer is you won't until you become aware and guide yourself in a conscious living direction. For me, I have become so aware of the influence of images on my subconscious mind that, most of the time, I avoid any TV shows or movies with violence and depressing subjects. It takes me awhile to shake their impact on my conscious mind, and I know they are still in my subconscious mind, because I often dream about them days later. For times that I want to stay current on the news of the world, I only listen to Pacifica Radio and National Public Radio, where at least I know that the stories are factual and are unfiltered by corporate interests. But I still only listen for a brief period of time, and when I feel like the weight of the world is becoming too much, I turn it off. Your experiences are programming your life twenty-four hours a day!

Have you ever noticed that we are our own worst enemy? We are harder on ourselves than anyone else ever could be? Start to notice the things you say to yourself throughout your day. When you wake up and look in the mirror, are you saying, "Hello, beautiful, today is going to be a great day!" or "I look so tired and old, my best days are behind me"? When you are getting dressed, do you say, "I look like a hot mama!" or "I am so out of shape and I look terrible"? When you are on your way to work, do you say, "I am a strong leader and I will set a great example today" or "I hate my job, this is such a grind and I hope everyone will just stay away today"? Start to pay attention to the words you use with yourself. Words have so much power; they are literally programming your brain to believe what you are telling it. Now that you know the power of your words, you can begin the process of reprogramming your brain with loving, kind, optimistic affirmations all day long. When you notice a negative thought, imagine Miss Pac-Man coming to eat it! Once she eats the thought, replace it with a positive, reinforcing thought, such as, "I am worthy and wonderful exactly as I was created."

Okay, now let's go back to the relationship between the conscious and subconscious mind. Now we understand that the greater the alignment, the more likely you are to succeed. As Joseph Murphy explains in *The Power of the Subconscious Mind*,

> "An excellent way to get acquainted with the two functions of your mind is to look upon your own mind as a garden. You are a gardener, and you are planting seeds (thoughts) in your subconscious mind all day long, based on your habitual thinking. As you sow in your subconscious mind, so shall you reap in your body and environment."

So when you set the intention with your conscious mind to meet a fantastic man within a year and be in a committed relationship, you also have to surround yourself with reinforcing people, images and thoughts to create the momentum for this goal to manifest for you. You create the goal, but then you have to do your part by taking action to get to know your subconscious mind, to attain the results you want to achieve. The same holds true for the effect of your mind on your body.

Questions:

1. What self-defeating messages do you have in your subconscious mind?

____
____
____
____
____
____

2. What positive thoughts and affirmations can you replace the negative ones with?

____
____
____
____
____
____

"The secret of health for both mind and body is not to mourn for the past, not to worry about the future, or to anticipate troubles, but to live in the moment wisely and earnestly."

-Buddha

Be Present. Create the Life of Your Dreams Now! Live for This Moment

Life Lesson #13:

If you think about it, all we really have is this moment we are living in. While we are in this moment, we often are not present to enjoy it. We are either thinking about the past, which is gone and cannot be changed, or thinking about the future, which is out of our control. When we arrive at that point in the future, it will be "now." In *Wherever You Go, There You Are*, Jon Kabat-Zinn reminds us that "Our lives unfold only in moments. If we are not fully present for many of those moments, we may not only miss what is most valuable in our lives but also fail to realize the richness and depth of our possibilities for growth and transformation." Often we are so preoccupied with regret about the past and anxiety and fear about the future that we fail to realize that the present is all that we have. If we want to address the issues of the past and manifest the future we desire, we have to be alive and active in the present moment. If we approach each moment as the only one, we are more apt to deem it precious and use it wisely. We are inclined to have authentic connections and valuable moments, because we are tuned in to the fact that this moment is all they can truly impact.

Releasing the burden of the past and the unknown of the future, and instead focusing on the here and now, is a valuable tool. We should move away from looking at our past, other than the broad themes and patterns. It is not helpful for us to wallow in our childhood issues, failed relationships and unfulfilled financial and professional opportunities. By doing so, we focus on the negative feelings of sadness, fear, inadequacy and low self-esteem, which only lead to more of the same feelings and outcomes. While thinking about long-term goals is helpful, it is distracting and paralyzing to focus on the unknown future questions of "What will happen when?" and "What if?" and "How do I know?" These are questions that we all share, but there is no way to see the future. The closest way to do so is to think about where we are at right now, in this moment, and what we want to feel, see and hear in the future. By focusing on these things, we can create a plan, with action steps that will occur in the present and accountability, which will get us where we want to be in the future. By staying present in the moment, you can concentrate on the task at hand and the step you are trying to accomplish at this time. The actions you take in the present are the actions that will create the future you want. So if you can stay focused and conscious in the moment, you can effectively eliminate the negative feelings of the past and the uncertainty of the future—by knowing that you are actively creating the life you want right now!

It is important to let go of the past and move forward. Hold on to valuable lessons, but release your attachment to certain outcomes and beliefs, and instead allow forgiveness of others and yourself, as well as acceptance of where you are now, to take the lead in your life. This transformation is integral to experiencing the fullness of the life you are destined to experience. Deepak Chopra explains this so beautifully:

> "If you have your attention on what is, see its fullness in every moment, you will discover the dance of the divine in every leaf, in every petal, in every blade of grass, in every rainbow, in every rushing stream, in every breath of every living being. [...]Beyond memory and judgment lies the ocean of universal consciousness."

Questions:

1. How will you feel when you release the obstacles, challenges and hardships of the past?

____

____

____

____

____

____

2. In this moment, what are you experiencing?

____

____

____

____

____

____

"People deal too much with the negative, with what is wrong. Why not try to see positive things, to just touch those things and make them bloom?"

-Thich Nhat Hanh

Shift to a Positive Mental Attitude

Life Lesson #14:

We have all heard the saying, "Are you a glass-half-full or a glass-half-empty person?" Well, I used to be a glass-half-empty person, and now I am a glass-half-full person. I encourage you to make the shift for yourself. I changed my outlook by understanding the power of my subconscious mind, and through my increased faith in a power greater than myself. I realized that my reality is shaped by the thoughts I have all day long. The more we think about negative things, the more negative things are attracted into our lives. We also begin to be negative and see negativity all around. Just writing these sentences, I am feeling a shift in my energy; it just feels bad.

We can shift this experience by waking up in a good mood, focusing on how the day is going to be great and reminding ourselves that fabulous experiences are on their way. As Marianne Williamson encourages us, "We can always choose to perceive things differently. We can focus on what's wrong in our life, or we can focus on what's right." This process activates our subconscious mind to work to make these things come true. Very quickly, our day begins to move forth in a positive light with meaningful interactions. When we approach our day and moments with a positive mental attitude, we set the tone for all around us, and we begin to find the good in every situation. In *Success Through a Positive Mental Attitude*, Napoleon Hill defines *"Positive Mental Attitude"* in this way:

> "A Positive Mental Attitude is the right mental attitude. What is the right mental attitude? It is most often comprised of the 'plus' characteristics symbolized by such words as faith, integrity, hope, optimism, courage, initiative, generosity, tolerance, tact, kindliness and good common sense. A person with positive mental attitude aims for high goals and constantly strives to achieve them."

We have the inner strength and power to change the way we see the world and the way we feel about our lives. By focusing on the positive, we call forth all of the powers of the universe to work together with us to manifest our dreams.

Questions:

1. Think about a recent setback or obstacle. What is the silver lining and positive takeaway you can find in the experience?

2. How will your Positive Mental Attitude impact those around you at home and at work, as well as yourself?

"You can have anything you want if you want it desperately enough. You must want it with an exuberance that erupts through the skin and joins the energy that created the world."

-Sheila Graham

Aim High, Don't Sell Yourself Short

Life Lesson #15:

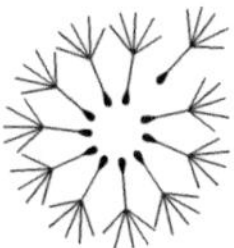

Far too often we play it safe. We are taught early on that we are overconfident or full of ourselves to want it all. The problem is that the part of ourselves that dreamed big is the part that we are missing now. The old higher-self thought outside of the box, was creative and optimistic about life. The new lower-self is safe, scared, bored and unhappy. So I encourage you to start digging deep and thinking about your life. Where you are now does not limit you from where you want to go. Begin to think of your largest goals and dreams in all of the areas of your life. They may not come to fruition immediately, but if you know where you want to go, you can make a plan to get there. As Oprah Winfrey says, "Every time you state what you want or believe, you're the first to hear it. It's a message to both you and others about what you think is possible. Don't put a ceiling on yourself."

As women we are used to putting everyone else's needs before our own. Many of us became caregivers early in life, as a caregiver for our younger siblings, parents or grandparents. We learned how to meet everyone's expectations of us. We tried to hit the mark in school while still having heavy demands at home. Then, in relationships, we take the lead with organizing, planning and day-to-day operation of the logistics. In our homes, we not only work but feel responsible to cook, clean, be happy, beautiful and sexy. This is a lot to handle, especially while not reaching high for our own needs. Often in the workplace, women don't take credit for our work, or we give the credit to our team. Meanwhile, our male counterparts have no problem receiving praise for their hard work and accomplishments. When it comes to promotion, women often don't ask for what we deserve, and we wait for the acknowledgement to come to us, which it often never does. When looking for a new job, we underestimate our experience and qualifications and often don't apply for higher-end jobs with more pay and benefits, because we don't deem ourselves worthy. This madness needs to stop!

The same way we encourage everyone who we care for to live their lives to the fullest and chase their dreams; we have to do the same. It is not enough to meet your life halfway; you need to go all-out and reach your top. This does not mean in terms of title and income; it means you need to figure out what you want out of your life and go after it. Go big! Napoleon Hill reminds us in *Think and Grow Rich* that "all who succeed in life get off to a bad start, and pass through many heartbreaking struggles before they 'arrive.' The turning point in the lives of those who succeed usually comes at the moment of some crisis, through which they are introduced to their 'other selves.'"

If your dream is to compete in marathons, then don't be satisfied with your goal being to run twice a week. Start to identify the steps it takes to run a marathon, make a plan to get to that point and take the first step in that direction. Aim high with your goals. If you work hard toward them and you don't hit your mark, that is fine—you will probably still be at a better place than you would have been if you'd devalued yourself and set easy, safe goals. When we are on our deathbed, we don't want to have any regrets. We want to feel like we lived a life full of love, purpose and adventure, and that we gave it our best. No one wants to feel like they wasted their life, oblivious to their true purpose and blind to the full potential of their being. Instead, dream big and go for it!

Questions:

1. What big dreams do you want to achieve?

____

____

____

____

____

____

2. What is your plan for achieving them?

____

____

____

____

____

____

"It is never too late to be what you might have been."

-George Eliot

Imagine the Life You Desire, and Set Big Goals to Achieve

Life Lesson #16:

I can't say enough how important it is to have clarity of vision around the goals for your life. The universe wants to deliver these things to you, but if you do not have clarity of your intentions, then the universe does not know what direction to send you toward. Setting short and long-term goals for your life in all areas—personal, professional, financial, spiritual, in relationships, community service, etcetera—creates clarity for your direction and helps you create an action plan to get there. Start with the big goals for the next twelve months in the areas of your life you want to focus on developing, and then brainstorm the action steps it will take to get there.

Let's say you have a goal to complete the first draft of your memoir in the next twelve months. You want to construct a plan of all the action steps you need to take to get there over these twelve months. Start with all of the broad strokes, and then figure out which order they go in. To write your memoir, you may want to create an outline of your book, figuring out the chapter titles, content and supporting subcategories. Then you may want to set up deadlines for yourself at the three, six and nine-month marks with certain productivity checkpoints associated with each time frame. Maybe at three months you will want to have completed five chapters and twenty-five thousand words. Then you have to break that down into smaller increments and set yourself daily and weekly goals so you can hit your mark. You may look at how much time per day you will write and how much writing you want to produce. This is reverse engineering from the twelve-month goal all the way backward to the daily goal.

The more specific you are with the action steps you are going to take, the more accountability you create, which leads to you accomplishing the results you set out to achieve. This formula applies to all goals you have for yourself. Set your long-term goal, and then work backward from the last action steps needed to accomplish the goal. You are creating the blueprint to follow in order to reach your dreams. Create the dreams, create an action plan to achieve them, and then take action on them. It is a simple formula, which, once embraced, can transform your life. As Sarah Ban Breathnach, in *Simple Abundance: A Daybook for Comfort and Joy*, reminds us, "Dreams are gifts of the Spirit meant to alter us. Trust that the same power that gifted you with your dream knows how to help you make it come true."

Questions:

1. What is one twelve-month goal you want to achieve?

____
____
____
____
____
____

2. What action steps do you need to accomplish at the three, six, nine and twelve-month marks to achieve it?

____
____
____
____
____
____

"Intuition is a spiritual faculty, and does not explain, but simply points the way."

-Florence Scovel Shinn

Listen to Your Intuition, the Inner Voice Giving You Ideas, and Take Action

Life Lesson #17:

Every idea we have is a product of divine inspiration flowing through us. We all have light bulb moments, when a creative idea or thought flashes into our mind and we know that this idea needs to be introduced to the world. Remember that ideas need to be protected to grow strong, so do not share your ideas with anyone until you have determined how you feel about it and what you want to do with it. Sharing your idea too early makes you vulnerable to others' input and can kill your idea in its infancy. Any fear, anxiety or confusion you may be processing will only be heightened by talking to people about your idea too soon. In Tyndale's *100 Great Ideas to Relax and Reduce Stress*, it is noted that,

> "While reality checks are good and a necessary part of being successful, it takes dreams and the ability to continue dreaming to creatively change and shape reality. Dreaming allows you to invent new pathways, attempt new things, and revise the way you do things. Dreams express the desires of your heart, desires that may be the whisper of God's Spirit telling you what's possible and achievable."

During the early stages of an idea and dream, you want to cultivate the idea and build your passion and faith in it. Then only share it with a select few, telling them you don't need their advice or opinion but, instead, their support in bringing the idea to fruition.

Now, the key is taking action on it. We have all had many great ideas that we have not acted on, and down the line we saw that someone else had the same idea and did take the action and was rewarded for it. Once a thought is created, it is introduced into the common universe of thought, and it is out there floating around. If you do not take action, someone else will have the thought and will take action. Obviously, not all ideas are good ideas, but that is where the beginning stages of growing the idea help you to determine whether it is a good one. Are you passionate about it? Will it be of service to others? Can you see yourself investing time and money into the fruition of the idea? If you answered yes to all of these questions, then start making a plan from conception to execution of the idea.

Figure out the specific action steps to manifest your vision. Then take action! With one baby step and then another, focus on the step that is right in front of you—not what you have to do next week, month or year. Focusing on the action step you are taking right now will keep you grounded, confident and conscious. It doesn't matter what will happen on step twelve if you are still on step three. You have to give all of your attention to the completion of the current task, so that the lessons you are learning on this step will inform the direction in which you go for the next one, and so on.

If you have a great idea and are full of passion about it, act on it. If you don't, someone else will. If you feel lost about your purpose, go back to all those unfulfilled ideas you have had over the years. It is likely you were not aware at the time that those ideas were created to lead you in the direction you were destined to go. Don't fight the signs; follow them and your life will begin to have more flow, harmony and purpose.

Questions:

1. What do you hear your intuition telling you?

____
____
____
____
____
____

2. What great ideas do you have on the back burner that you haven't taken action on?

____
____
____
____
____
____

"A new life will come forth from the womb of darkness."

-Na'im Akbar

Failure Is an Opportunity Designed Just for You

Life Lesson #18:

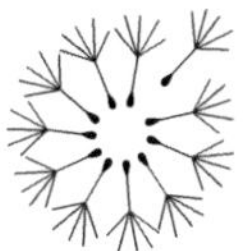

For some reason, we have been programmed to believe that if we attempt something and don't achieve it, then it is a failure, which is a bad thing. This feeling of being a failure is extremely destructive and can eat away at our self-esteem. We have all heard the saying "It is better to have tried and failed than never to have tried at all." Well, many people are frozen in life by the fear of failure. What is the big deal with failure? So you made an attempt to reach a goal and fell short? So what? You are not your actions, you are not your accomplishments, and they do not define you. You are the beautiful, complete soul that will be one hundred percent whole no matter how many "failures" you have. As Napoleon Hill challenges us in *Think and Grow Rich*, "if the one thing you wish to do is right, and you believe in it, go ahead and do it! Put your dreams across, and never mind what 'they' say and if you meet with temporary defeat, for 'they,' perhaps, don't know that *every failure brings with it the seeds of an equivalent success*"—or even greater!

Most of us sit in two camps. First, there are those who want to control every aspect of their lives and image. They are the ones who would rather play it safe in life, basically not challenging themselves to grow, because they would prefer to be bored, unfulfilled and look good on the outside rather than to take a risk and be a "failure." The other camp of people takes risks and challenges themselves, but when they fall short of their goals, they become self-destructive, constantly ruminating over the mistakes they made and what they should have done different. The common ground between these two groups is the lack of consciousness of the experience and the lessons to learn from them.

Although it is comfortable to stay in one of these two places, I challenge you to see the silver lining in failure. Your life is all about having experiences and learning from them. If you stunt your growth and limit yourself to a "safe" life, you will not have rich experiences, and you will not learn the lessons that were created for you. If you take risks but then focus on the failure, then you are missing the boat. The key here is in the silver lining, which is that these failures were brought to you so you can understand the lessons from them. Then you can move forward, creating new opportunities, building on the blocks you've gained from the insight of your experiences. As Les Brown points out in *It's Not Over Until You Win!*, "After you have been knocked down or pushed by life, you should acknowledge the setback, understand why it happened, and then make a leap ahead of where you were when you were hit." Someone who has never been knocked down will not be as strong as someone who has been knocked down time and time again and keeps getting up stronger, ready to go again.

Stop living in fear of failure. This is your ego getting in the way. It is the part of you that believes you are defined by your accomplishments and your material wealth. It is your biggest enemy. When you become aware of how your ego sabotages you, you can recognize yourself going to the dark side, and you can remind yourself that there is a gem of a lesson in this failure that you can build on. This setback is only going to help you grow in the ways you are supposed to so you will be prepared when the opportunity created just for you arrives. Iyanla Vanzant reminds us that, "Challenges come so we can grow and be prepared for things we are not equipped to handle now. When we face our challenges with faith, prepared to learn, willing to make changes and, if necessary, to let go, we are demanding our power be turned on."

Questions:

1. What lessons can you learn from your latest obstacle or setback?

____
____
____
____
____
____

2. How does your fear of failure limit the potential of your life?

____
____
____
____
____
____

"We are most deeply asleep at the switch when we fancy we control any switches at all."

-Annie Dillard

Stop Pushing Your Life, Allow It to Unfold

Life Lesson #19:

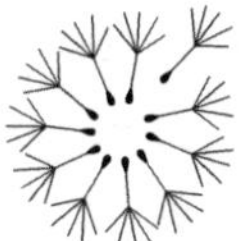

Sometimes we are so eager for our life to be a certain way and for changes to occur that we push our lives. We think if we dot every "i" and cross every "t" and search for every opportunity, then it will all fall into place and we will have the life of our dreams. The problem with this approach is that when we are pushing our lives to move forward, we are not allowing the natural rhythm of our life to occur. We get in our own way! In *Simple Abundance: A Daybook of Comfort and Joy*, Sarah Ban Breathnach explains,

> "Personal growth also comes in spasms: three steps forward, two steps back, and then a long plateau when it seems nothing is happening. But it's important to realize that this dormant period always seems to precede a growth spurt. Unfortunately, during the dormant period, we very often become depressed and decide to give up. [...] Each day offers us a gift if we only look for it."

When we are pushing our lives forward, we are not present in the moment to learn the lessons along the way and see the beauty around ourselves. We have tunnel vision to get where we want in life, but we are passing up the amazing people and experiences along the way. We don't realize that these moments are what our lives are all about. As they say, "life is about the journey, not the destination." There is a rhythm to life—like the ocean, the currents of our life go up and down, each time growing with the knowledge of the journey. When you push your life, you disrupt the natural sequence of things, missing steps and creating weaknesses. If you can't recognize the teachers, learn from the lessons and grow from the experiences, you won't be ready when the opportunities present themselves.

Most of us hate to be told to relax, but I am coming from a place of love. Relax. It is okay. Everything is going to be fine. As women, that is all we really want to hear. We want the comfort of knowing that there is a master plan at work. And there is. You are the lead in the play of your life. You can do the best job possible playing your part, but you have to let the universe direct you. If you can't receive the cues and modifications, then you will give a subpar performance. I know we all want desperately to knock this life out of the park. But when we are scared, when we are desperate, when we are controlling, we stand in the way of our greatness unfolding naturally. Do yourself a favor and stop pushing life forward. Get out of your own way, and lead with faith in yourself and a power greater than you. This moment is here just for you. There is no better moment to come than the one you have right now. Be at peace, and trust that you are moving along just as you are supposed to, right on time for all things. As Deepak Chopra reminds us,

> "The way of peace is a soul journey. [...]If you can live from the level of your soul, you are doing something very special. The important thing is how much consciousness you add to the whole

of human existence, for that is how eternity expresses itself, like a lamp shining through the window of eternity."

Questions:

1. How can you relieve the pressure on yourself and practice self-care?

____
____
____
____
____
____

2. What is great about your life right now?

____
____
____
____
____
____

"Mothering myself has become a way of listening to my deepest needs, and of responding to them while I respond to my inner child."

-Annie Dillard

You Teach Others How to Treat You

Life Lesson #20:

Many of us grow up hearing that we are princesses, and that we should be treated by others like we are a princess or a queen. However, often those in our lives do not treat us very well at all. It is easy to put the blame on others for the way they treat us, but in reality, the blame falls squarely on our shoulders. If we don't love ourselves, how can we expect others to do the same? When we have low self-esteem, we don't demand love and respect from those around us; we take what we get, and we complain about it without realizing that we are allowing the treatment. When we begin to feel worthy and build our confidence, we hold others to a higher standard. We no longer tolerate abuse, neglect and dysfunction and instead settle for no less than healthy, supportive and loving relationships. When you face someone treating you badly, let them know that you do not deserve that treatment and will not tolerate it. If they can't treat you kindly, then you will have to move on to those who can.

You will see over time that if you show more love to yourself and hold higher expectations for those in your life, those around you will either start to adjust their behavior or you will have to let them go. As your circle expands with people who support your highest good, those who do not will stand out. It will be easy to zero in on those who bring drama and chaos into your life and to let them go. Everyone grows at a different pace; we are all on our own journeys. But as you shed your layers to reveal your most beautiful, shiny self, you may need to create distance with those who are not moving forward on their own journeys. You want to surround yourself with people who are interested in self-growth and a mentally and physically healthy life. They don't need to have the same goals as you or be moving as fast as you, but they have to want to be their best. Not everyone is ready to do the work, which is their struggle to bear, but you can't be tied down by those who prefer to remain stuck in dysfunction. Remember, if you are mad at the way someone is treating you, turn the situation back on yourself, and make the adjustments necessary to change the situation.

Questions:

1. What dysfunctional relationships do you have in your life?

____
____
____
____
____
____

2. How can you express your expectations to those around you?

____
____
____
____
____
____

"When we truly care for ourselves, it becomes possible to care more profoundly about other people. The more alert and sensitive we are to our own needs, the more loving and generous we can be towards others."

-Eda LeShan

Ask for What You Want

Life Lesson #21:

Women often feel unappreciated, unrecognized and exhausted. We feel like we are constantly juggling everyone else's needs without anyone taking note of all of our hard work. We think, *How hard would it be for someone else to do the dishes? Or, Is it too much to ask to run me a bubble bath and rub my feet?* Or, *How about a "thank you for all you do for me and our family—we are so grateful for everything!"* When we don't receive these affirmations, it can lead to anger, resentment, low self-esteem and depression. These states of mind impact all those around us by manifesting as a less-patient and short-tempered mom or an exhausted and emotionally and sexually unavailable partner. After all the work we do, it sucks to be received in a negative light by our kids and loved ones.

We expect for others to read our minds and know just what we need, since we think we can anticipate all the needs of those we care for. Why can't they do it for us? Well, the fact of the matter is they just can't, and the sooner we understand that, the closer we will be to getting what we want. Not everyone shares our gifts of mind reading and anticipation of needs; these are the special tools we were created with. Instead of being resentful that these skills are not reciprocated our way, we need to ask for what we want. I know, asking for what you want takes the fun out of it. We shouldn't have to ask for what we need; the people around us are supposed to know. But now that we have determined they just don't know how to do that, we need to make the adjustment to improve our quality of life.

Our partners and spouses have no problem asking for what they want and taking care of their needs when they come up. They are usually masters at comforting themselves with material things, entertainment and relaxation. However, we stand as martyrs trying to put the needs of our families before our own. We think about how every decision we make with time and money will impact everyone else. In general it is a good quality, but we are no good to anyone if we are the angry, whining, pissed-off versions of ourselves. It is also not good modeling for our children. We want nothing more than for our kids to be healthy, well-adjusted adults who do not make our mistakes. We want for them to have high self-worth and to express their feelings and take care of themselves physically, mentally and emotionally. How can we expect them not to follow in our footsteps if we are modeling a bad attitude toward ourselves and others? This can all change by understanding that you need to take charge of your life. No one can do it but you. Iyanla Vanzant reminds us in her book *In the Meantime: Finding Yourself and the Love You Want:* "You have set standards for how you want to be treated and what you expect from yourself and for yourself."

If you want your life to be a certain way—for you to spend your time doing certain things, for your family to help with certain tasks—you have to figure out what those things are and to express your needs and intentions to your family. For example, if you need more romance in your life, you may need to take the lead with the planning. Pick a regular date night, find a babysitter, figure out what you want to do and tell your loved one to show up. If you need more help around the house, have a family meeting and write down all of the tasks that need to be done in the house. Have all those who are capable of helping select the tasks that they can do. Also, if you need help with housework or childcare, look at your household budget with your spouse and figure out how to squeeze out a little money for a housekeeper once a month and additional childcare help. Investing money into your peace of mind will exponentially grow into more love, patience and connection with your family. If you make yourself a priority, express your needs and get in the driver's seat about making them happen, all those around you will follow suit.

An example of this from my life is that my husband has no problem taking care of his needs. If he feels stressed or wakes up with aches and pains, the next day he will get a massage. His passion is refereeing basketball. During basketball season, he is away a few nights a week to pursue his dreams. I have learned that, instead of being resentful with him for taking care of himself, I have to be more like him. So when I need a spa day or a ladies' night out, instead of thinking about what bill I could pay with that money, I invest in myself. Also, when I want to take an additional course to further my knowledge and career, I try not to concern myself with being away from the kids and remind myself that I will be a happier, more present mom if I fulfill my needs and give back to myself. Don't get me wrong, it is a challenge to do, but it is like any muscle: You have to exercise it for it to become stronger. The more I push myself to take care of my needs, the easier it becomes, and everyone adjusts accordingly. I know my husband will go for what he needs, so I have to go for it too—and so do you!

I suggest we all create a "comfort tool kit" full of surefire things we know we can do when we need a little stress release, recharge of our batteries or pampering. For example, these are the things in my comfort tool kit: English Breakfast tea; red wine; bagels and lox; sushi; scented candles; Feist or Adele music; a lit fire; reality TV; foot massages; hiking; connecting with nature; and hanging out with my sister. These are the things, when I am down, that I know I can turn to for comfort and to help me feel better. We all have days when we need a boost, and it helps to know easy things you can turn to that will bring you peace of mind. As Oprah Winfrey says, "If you neglect to recharge a battery, it dies. And if you run full-speed ahead without stopping for water, you lose momentum to finish the race." We need to finish the race for ourselves and for all of those that we care for.

Questions:

1. What needs do you have that your spouse or children can help with?

____
____
____
____
____
____

2. How can you spend a few hours a week taking care of yourself?

____
____
____
____
____
____

3. What things are in your “comfort tool kit”?

____
____
____
____
____
____

"The road to happiness lies in two simple principles: find what it is that interests you...and when you find it, put your whole soul into it - every bit of energy and natural ability you have."

-John D. Rockefeller

Live Your Life for You, Not for Others

Life Lesson #22:

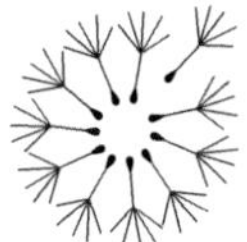

So many of us fall into the trap of living our lives for others and not for ourselves. Sometimes others' expectations and needs are so ingrained in our minds that we completely forget what we want and need. This often starts early in childhood. Many of us grew up with some level of dysfunction in our households. If there was an absent parent or a parent with an addiction, as children, we wanted to help our parents, and we filled the void that was lacking. We may have tried really hard to be perfect at school and at home so we wouldn't give our parents anything to be upset about. We may have taken on many household tasks so we could relieve the burden on our parents.

Later in life, we may have begun working earlier than is ideal to be able to help support the family. Going to college and getting a job often carry so much weight, because we are carrying the dreams and expectations of family members who were not able to achieve their own goals. You may say to your parents, "I really love dance and want to major in it." They may respond, "You can't major in dance, there are no jobs in dance! You should be a lawyer, doctor or dentist; these are good-paying jobs with a lot of security." These conversations from childhood all the way through adulthood impact us, altering our course and pushing us to live our lives for the wants and needs of others instead of ourselves. As Ivy Haley reminds us in *Discovering Your Purpose*,

> "When you blindly follow 'shoulds' and 'oughts' because you haven't determined your own purpose, you'll sense that you are compromising yourself. The days may range from slightly dull to downright boring as you zigzag along, buffeted by circumstances. How many people do you know who are in jobs or careers because they thought that's what they 'should' be doing? Often the 'shoulds' are layered across our imagination, blocking our creative ability to determine our truest passion and unearth our deepest desires. What a price we pay for them!"

The world can be a scary place. It is understandable that we all strive for security and that our parents want nothing but for us to be safe. Many people are out of work and cannot find a job. But the search for safety and security can come at a price. You have a song that you were born to sing, and you don't want to die with the music left inside of you. If you take a certain major, get a certain job, marry a certain spouse, live in a certain city because of the influences of those around you and the programming you receive, you are not living an authentic life for yourself, and ultimately, you will not be happy.

You can carry on the charade for a nice long time, but there comes a day, hopefully sooner than later, when you wake up and you don't recognize your life. It is incongruent with the vision you always had for yourself. Allow yourself the meltdown, and then pick yourself up. Understand that this is the greatest gift you have given yourself. You have now become aware that you are living your life for others instead of for yourself. It is never too late to turn things around in the direction of your intentions. Dig deep and do a personal inventory. What about your life do you like? What feels authentic to you? What don't you like? What feels like a burden to you? Once you figure out these things, you can create a plan, putting one foot in front of the other, moving forward in your journey for an authentic, fulfilling life.

Questions:

1. What about your life do you like, that feels authentic to you?

____
____
____
____
____
____

2. What don't you like about your life, which feels like a burden?

____
____
____
____
____
____

"Call it a clan, call it a network, call it a tribe, call it a family. Whatever you call it, whoever you are, you need one."

-Jane Howard

Remove Yourself From Toxic People, Energy Drainers and Negative Influences

Life Lesson #23:

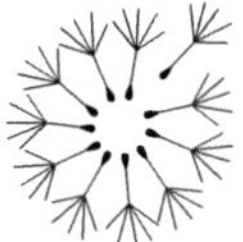

We all have people in our lives that we know are toxic, energy drainers and negative influences, and are not good for us. They usually ask for more than they give and are happy for things to stay status quo. These are the friends you call to tell about your latest opportunity who can always find something negative to say about it. They shoot holes in your ideas, undermine your goals and want you all to themselves. Derrick Sweet warns in *Healthy, Wealthy and Wise*,

> "Stay far away from negative influences—especially those that try to convince you that it is impossible to achieve dreams. We all have these thieves in our lives. By no means am I suggesting you dump your friends or well-intentioned relatives; just be aware that it is uncomfortable for some to watch you achieve more than them. It makes them realize that they are not living their lives to the fullest."

You are playing a role for them that they need, and they don't want to let you go for fear that you will see them for who they really are. I am telling you to release all of the people in your life who are not there for your highest good; I am telling you to be aware. When you get that feeling in your gut that something is off—that feeling of resentment or fear—pay attention to it. Your body is not lying to you. It is sending you signs that you need to pay attention to. The more you wake up to the signs, the better equipped you are to analyze your life and those in it. You will be more conscious of the friends and family members who always ask you to watch their kids, to pick something up at the pharmacy, to lend them your car or pay their bill—but when you need something or someone to talk to, they are nowhere to be found.

As you begin to step into your light and live your life authentically in greatness, the thorns in your side will stick out. You will have to make choices that support your healthy life. You will have to lay down healthy boundaries. It is fine to want to help people; that is a great quality. The problem becomes when your helping of others is not the result of you really wanting to and is not reciprocated. Once you have become aware of the disparity, the next time something is requested of you, make sure it is something you want to do, and that to do so will not be detrimental to your own life and the things you want to achieve. If it is, you need to say no. You don't need to give an explanation of why; you just say, "I am unavailable to do that today." Slowly, as you create healthy boundaries, those around you will get in line or phase themselves out. It is a natural progression once you empower yourself with taking care of yourself first.

If the people around you cannot be supportive and loving, you need to remove yourself from their influence and speak up to tell them that their statements do not resonate with you, and that they are not a good fit with the true essence of who you are and who you want to be. You can respond by letting them know all the great things that you think about yourself, and by showing them the love you have for yourself. Over time, this should help to eradicate their unkind actions and words, and if it doesn't, you need to take care of yourself and keep moving on.

You will also find that the more aware, open and authentic you are, the more the universe will send like-minded people into your life. Surround yourself with people who support you in your journey for happiness and who also want to grow, evolve and blossom. These are the people on whom you can focus your time and energy. The more you foster these relationships, the more your life will become aligned with the intentions you have for it.

Questions:

1. Who are the toxic, dysfunctional and negative people in your life?

____
____
____
____
____
____

2. How can you change the relationships and create healthy boundaries to limit their influence on your life?

____
____
____
____
____
____

"It is not death that a man should fear, but he should fear never beginning to live."

-Marcus Aurelius

Be Open and Vulnerable - It Is Better to Live a Life of Adventure Than of Safety

Life Lesson #24:

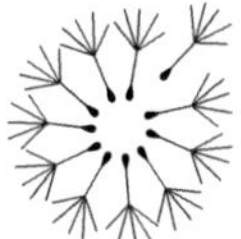

Whatever your belief system, when you think about the purpose of life, you probably agree that it has something to do with living it to the fullest and embracing all of the experiences life sends you. The purpose of life is clearly not about protecting ourselves from pain, rejection and judgment by living a safe life. You hear so often that people who have been hurt by their loved ones are protecting themselves from ever being hurt that way again. Well, why don't they just go jump off a bridge? Because they are effectively saying they are going to stop living. As the saying goes, many of us live until seventy-five but die at twenty-five. Do you want to be the person who stops living at twenty-five to be "safe" and is dead inside until you die? I don't think so—you wouldn't be reading this book if you were.

Life is about taking risks, making ourselves vulnerable and learning from the experience. The outcome may not always fall in our favor, but the outcome can be used to our advantage to learn about ourselves and to grow stronger and wiser. That is not to say that it is not scary and that our fears will not rise up, but we can use our wisdom to quiet those fears and be assured that, whatever the outcome, we will be fine. There is nothing wrong with a safe life, but "safe" is not congruent with greatness, imagination, creativity, passion and abundance. I know you want all of that, and I want it for you. That is why I am encouraging you to go for it. Open yourself up to all the possibilities of this lifetime. You can always console your ego if you fall short of your intentions, but you will know so much more for the next time around. Love is such a magical thing and feels so good. Granted, it hurts when your heart gets broken, but it is worth it. When I am old and gray, I want to be the little old lady in the rocking chair who says, "Honey, let me tell you about my life. I have had many loves, I have had much heartbreak, I have had many adventures, and I have had the best life." How about you? What do you want to say about your life?

Questions:

1. In what ways can you be more vulnerable and adventurous?

2. In your eulogy, what do you want them to say about your life?

"I've always believed that one woman's success can only help another woman's success."

-Gloria Vanderbilt

There Is Enough for Everyone, You Do Not Need to Compete - Stay in Your Lane and Work on Yourself While Lifting Up Others

Life Lesson #25:

In the past five years, with the popularity of *The Secret* and other metaphysical studies, we have heard a lot about "manifesting abundance." The phrase sounds very esoteric, but in reality it is very simple. It is based on the principle that there is an unlimited possibility and opportunity in the universe. There is also the indigenous expression "Buen vivir," which means there is just enough for everyone to have a good life and live well—there is enough love, happiness, success and wealth to go around. However, we get programmed from an early age to believe we must compete against others for resources. We have to be better than everyone else academically, intellectually, domestically and physically to attain our dreams, and if we aren't, the opportunity is going to someone else who is better than us. This way of thinking is so limiting and goes against human nature. There are many countries that take more than their share at the cost of other countries. This causes high infant-mortality rates and climate change, and it makes many large areas unlivable. Cooperation is the only way for all of us to experience the "Buen vivir" (the good life).

The only things that this type of competition creates are individualism, superiority, prejudice and judgment. Is that the kind of person you want to be or the kind of world you want to live in? It does not have to be a dog-eat-dog world; we only think it does because that is what we have been told since we were kids. In fact, the world is full of resources, opportunities and possibilities for all if we start looking for them. It takes a shift in perspective and a heightened awareness of the benefits of collaboration, partnership and mentorship. When we shift our perspective, we open ourselves up for the abundance to flow in. When the abundance comes, this is an opportunity to share with others and support them along their journeys to awareness. In reality we are not separate from each other; we are one. When one of us succeeds, we all succeed.

It is natural, because of our programming, to feel a sense of envy or jealousy when a friend or colleague attains something for which we are striving. But instead of allowing the negative, divisive thoughts to fester, recognize your thinking and shift them to thoughts of inspiration. As Michael Bernard Beckwith teaches, "There's enough for everyone. If you believe it, if you can see it, if you act from it, it will show up for you. That's the law." Now that you see someone living a life that you want, that is proof that it exists and that you too can achieve it. There is no shortage of love, happiness and opportunity. We live in a world of abundance and not lack, but it takes an effort to share the knowledge and opportunities so that we can all reach our dreams.

Questions:

1. Who in your life inspires you and can be your mentor?

2. Who can you inspire and be a mentor to?

"As long as you can find someone else to blame for anything you are doing, you cannot be held accountable or responsible for your growth or lack of it."

-Sun Bear

Take Responsibility for Your Choices and Actions, and Resist Self-Judgment

Life Lesson #26:

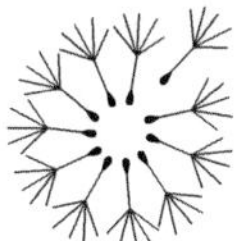

Why is it that we are our own harshest critics? There are plenty of people in the world who will criticize us and stand in judgment of us, so why do we do it to ourselves? We are constantly putting ourselves down for our appearance, limitations and lack of success, professionally and personally, instead of showing ourselves love. Imagine becoming aware of all the self-defeating actions we take and shifting to a place of love. We are doing the best we can, and as Oprah Winfrey says, "When you know better, you do better." So, in the moment, try to be as aware as possible and make the best choices you can. But if you fall short of your intentions or expectations, don't beat yourself up. You did your best, and now that you have learned from the experience, you will do better next time. You are not your actions; your soul is separate from them. Stop punishing yourself for things you cannot change. Move forward, being a better version of yourself now that you know better.

Keep in mind that you are the only one responsible for your choices; you cannot pass the responsibility on to others. It is too easy for us to blame other people for our poor choices, and we often do. But at the end of the day, we only have ourselves to hold responsible. Instead of blaming ourselves, we should search for the meaning in the lesson! There are hidden gems in everything if you look hard enough. You cannot put the responsibility of your life on others. You have to step up to the plate to figure it out. You can do this without knocking yourself down. You can do it with love.

When I say or do something I wish I hadn't, instead of mulling over the situation and continuing to break myself down, I look for the lesson. I dissect it. Okay, so maybe I did not handle that well. I can't go back and change it—I can only learn to do better moving forward. When I am faced with that situation again, I will do it differently. Les Brown reminds us in *Live Your Dreams*,

> "When you decide to pursue greatness, you are taking responsibility for your life. This means that you are choosing to accept the consequences of your actions, and to become the agent of your mental, physical, spiritual and material success. You may not be able to control what life puts in your path, but I believe you can always control who you are."

Be kind to yourself and have patience. We are not perfect and were not created to be perfect. If we were perfect, we would not be here. Humans are flawed, and that is the reason for this journey: to open ourselves up, learn from each other and become the best versions of our selves.

Questions:

1. When have you placed blame on others for the outcome of your choices?

____
____
____
____
____
____

2. What recent actions have you taken that you can learn from?

____
____
____
____
____
____

"If your spiritual philosophy is not moving you to the state of peace, health, wealth and love your spirit desires…you need a new spiritual philosophy."

-Sun Bear

Identify Your Values and Priorities, and You Will Know Where to Focus Your Time and Energy

Life Lesson #27:

It is important when creating your goals that you are clear on what your guiding principles and values are in life. Make a list of what values are most important to you in all the areas of your life. What qualities do you value and want to share with the world? Identifying these values and specifying how you will integrate them into your life helps guide your journey along the path that is important to you. It is helpful to identify your guiding values to align your actions with them. Ivy Haley states in *Discovering Your Purpose*,

> "We experience inner conflict when our behaviors oppose our values. If our decisions aren't aligned with our values, a sense of discomfort and uneasiness results. Psychologists call this phenomenon 'cognitive dissonance'—acting in a way that doesn't feel right. The process makes you feel squirmy inside; it goes against the grain. [...]You can generally tell whether your decisions are consistent with your values by your level of contentment. You have more peace of mind

when your behaviors align with your value structure. And being in harmony with your deepest values is essential to establish a sense of purpose and direction."

For example, within your relationships, you may identify that vulnerability, commitment and positivity are guiding principles for you. Therefore, when looking at your twelve-month goals for the area of relationships in your life, this will help you construct goals that mirror the qualities that are important for you. Your goals may be to create more intimacy and honesty in your love relationship by implementing a weekly share night, where you and your partner each share a story from your childhood that was important to you and discuss how that moment impacts your adult life. Also, you may set a goal to remove toxic girlfriends from your life and create a close circle of like-minded friends. You can take action on this by setting aside weekly time to call the friends you identified, with whom you want to grow closer. You can spend monthly one-on-one time with each friend to listen, be attentive and be thoughtful in the relationship. You can create a quarterly group meeting of these women, where you share your goals for the next quarter and give each other positive reinforcement and encouragement.

When you identify the guiding values that are important to you, you can align your goals with them. By doing so, you begin focusing your life with intentions, thoughts, feelings, actions, people and things that are all working together to move you forward in the direction that is for your highest good.

Questions:

1. What are guiding values for your life?

____

____

____

____

____

____

2. What goals can you create to foster these values?

____

____

____

____

____

____

"Time is the most valuable coin in your life. You and you alone will determine how that coin will be spent. Be careful that you don't let other people spend it for you."

-John Dryden

Understanding Your Many Identities Helps You Love All of Yourself

Life Lesson #28:

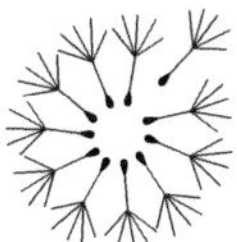

Women are so dynamic. As they say, "Women hold up half the sky." But in reality we are the backbone of the world. Women are contributing to the world twenty-four hours a day through our visible and invisible work. We were created with the maternal instinct to nurture others, as well as with the natural gift of juggling so many things at one time and performing well at all of them. On top of our natural gifts, we are programmed from an early age to understand the woman's role in society. We are expected to contribute financially to the household while also handling the brunt of the housework and cooking. Additionally, we are expected to be beautiful, in shape, delightful with a sunny disposition, and a doting woman to our partners. It is way more than any one woman can bear; however, we all feel that it is a standard we need to uphold. Many of us get very close to this standard to the detriment of caring for ourselves. We put all of our energy into working for someone else, or being a caregiver to our children and loved ones. After giving all we have to others, there is often not a lot left for ourselves.

Over time, neglect of our spirit, body and mind leads to resentment, sadness and anger. These are lethal emotions that we need to learn to move away from. One way to do so is to understand that you are a whole human being with different parts of yourself that need to be nurtured. If they are not, they will atrophy and die off. Before it is too late, love yourself back to health. Sarah Ban Breathnach points out in *Simple Abundance: A Daybook of Comfort and Joy,*

> "It takes peace of mind and clarity to recognize and reorder meaningful, personal priorities. Maybe that is why so many of us procrastinate. But the more our lives and attention spans are segmented by our children, our careers, our homes, our marriages and our needs for personal expression, the more we need to identify what is truly important in our lives."

To combat neglect of oneself, I suggest you always look at yourself, your goals and your intentions in a holistic way. Steven Covey has been very influential in my approach with what he refers to as our different "roles." You are not just a professional, or a wife, or a mother; you are all of that and more. If each week the goals you set and the actions you take are all in just a few areas of your life instead of all areas, then you are neglecting yourself. So start looking at your week and think, Who am I? Which areas of my life create the whole of me? For myself, I break it down like this. I am:

- Myself
- Mother
- Wife
- Financial/household manager
- Caregiver and friend
- Author and speaker
- Life coach and teacher

For each week, I look at each category of myself and think about the three most significant action steps I can take in that area of my life to move closer to my long-term goals for that zone. For example, my goals for the week look like this:

- Myself
    A. Meditate and pray for fifteen minutes daily in the A.M. and P.M.
    B. Run for thirty minutes three times a week, and go for a hike once
    C. Practice yoga for thirty minutes two times a week
- Mother
    A. Volunteer for two hours at kindergarten class
    B. Set up a play date for Sunday
    C. RSVP for birthday party
- Wife
    A. Set up date night
    B. Cook favorite meal on Thursday
    C. Help review Joe's résumé
- Financial/household manager
    A. Pay bills and balance checkbook
    B. Do laundry
    C. Do a food shop
- Caregiver and friend
    A. Pick up medications from the pharmacy for grandma
    B. Host a jewelry party for sister
    C. Write thank-you notes
- Author and speaker
    A. Attend one speaking engagement
    B. Write daily for sixty minutes
    C. Approve graphics for book cover
- Life coach and teacher
    A. Facilitate life-skills workshop for teens
    B. Facilitate one group coaching session by webinar
    C. Review mentee's ninety-day action plan

Once you have identified your intentions for the week in all of the important aspects of your life, immediately make appointments with yourself to do these things. Bust out your date book or smartphone, and figure out which day and time you will do which item, and block off the time. Also list the items for each day on the daily to-do list. Obviously, this is still a lot to accomplish for the week, but the difference is, when you approach it this way, you are in control of your time. You have identified what is important to you, what your long-term goals are and the areas of your life that define who you are.

Now your vision, long-term goals and action steps are all aligned with the same purpose of having the most inspired, purposeful and holistic life possible, led by you. If you fall short of completing all of the tasks, that is okay. Just try to do as many of the tasks as you can in all of the areas you identified, and by the end of the week, you will feel fantastic, because you will have completed the most important things in the most important areas of your life. You will not have neglected yourself; instead, you will have fed your spirit with the excitement of a life built on purpose and love for yourself.

Questions:

1. What are your different identities?

2. What are the two most important tasks you can accomplish within each identity this week?

"Concern yourself less with what you have than what you are, so that you can become as excellent as possible."

-Socrates

Your Value Is Not Measured by What You Have

Life Lesson #29:

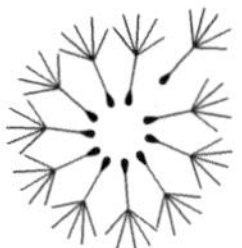

What a curse it is to grow up in a world that values money so greatly—in many cases, above anything else. Very early on, we are infected with the drive to attain material wealth through homes, cars, clothes and vacations. While these things are enjoyable, the constant drive to attain them all can be maddening. The cliché "Money does not make you happy" is debatable, but what is clear is it will not bring you lasting happiness if you are not already happy with yourself. Your pursuit of material things and wealth may actually burden you with undue stress and anxiety. Often when people accumulate all of their things, they then long for a "simple" life without the obligations, bills, paperwork and rat race required to keep it all going. As Eckhart Tolle states in *A New Earth,* "The unchecked striving for more, for endless growth, is a dysfunction and a disease. It is the same dysfunction the cancerous cell manifests, whose only goal is to multiply itself, unaware that it is bringing about its own destruction by destroying the organism of which it is a part."

Who you are is not measured by your bank balance but by your heart, mind, spirit and actions. You can be the poorest person with the richest life. Money and a good life do not go hand in hand. You must first apply all the life lessons and get to a state of self-love and inner peace before you can enjoy what money can offer. Then you may find that other things are more important to you. Instead of striving to keep up with the Joneses and their latest and greatest toys or vacations, find a mentor whom you can strive to keep up with in the way they live their life authentically and in service. The pursuit of happiness through service and purpose is much more likely to be attained than pursuing happiness through wealth. Just because people have shiny cars or beautiful homes does not mean they are not struggling inside. These are all distractions from looking within. It takes many people their whole lives to understand that none of their material things have anything to do with who they are. Don't fall victim to this trap. Instead, use your wisdom to overcome the temptations and teach others to do the same. Most of us know good financial practices, but we don't always heed them and implement them in our lives. For the sake of a reminder, I will mention the key practices that I find helpful:

- Live within your means. Say you make $2,000 a month; make a monthly budget of expenses and make sure that they do not go over the $2,000. If they do, make the necessary adjustments to your expenses to live within your means.

- Pay yourself first. Make sure that in your monthly budget, before you allocate all of your income, you set aside a portion for a six-month security fund, and put at least ten percent of your net income toward retirement savings. Then figure out your bills with the remaining amount of money.

- Don't take on unsecured debt. If you can't pay cash for it, you really don't need it or have the money to pay for it.

- If you need more money, find a way to earn more. Negotiate for a raise at work, take on a second job or start the small business you have been dreaming of. Have faith that the money will come. If you do what you love, the money will follow.

- Share a portion of your income with others. Give away some of your income to your church, charity or those in need. Not only is it important to help others when we can, but money carries energy with it. The more you give away, the stronger the energetic force becomes to bring more money back to you.

Questions:

1. If you strip away all of your material things, what are the things about yourself that you value most?

____

____

____

____

____

____

2. How much does your drive for money cause stress in your life?

____

____

____

____

____

____

3. What changes can you make to your relationship with money to create more balance, peace and gratitude?

____

____

____

____

____

____

"Grace fills empty spaces, but it can only enter where there is a void to receive it, and it is grace itself which makes this void."

-Simone Weil

Connecting With the Energy of the Universe and a Power Greater Than You Brings Comfort and Purpose

Life Lesson #30:

Many cultures, religions and societies around the world understand the importance and value of integrating spiritual practices into their daily lives as a method of staying connected to the universe and a higher power. However, in American society, we have fallen into the trap of the rat race and wake up already feeling behind schedule and pressed for time. When I wake up, I have to pack lunches, make breakfast, get the kids dressed, hair and teeth brushed and take them to school, all without a second to pay attention to myself. Fortunately, I became conscious that this cycle was depriving my soul of much-needed love, rejuvenation and focus. I learned how to implement the basic spiritual practices of meditation, deep breathing, prayer, affirmations, intentions and visualization into my daily life. Since I shifted my lifestyle to incorporate these essential practices, my life's purpose has revealed itself, and I continue to reach deeper levels of my authentic self. I urge you to experiment with these practices one by one and see what fits for you. There is no right or wrong way to do any of them; you can create a custom routine that feels good to you. The main thread here is to set aside a little time each day to center yourself, ground yourself and focus on a love of yourself and all things. As Michael Bernard Beckwith reminds us, "Meditation and prayer have withstood the test of time. They work today as perfectly as they did for those who first practiced and perfected them." The universe is holding you in its arms, wrapping you in love, and the more connected you are with this, the more fulfilling your life will become. Many of the different prayers, affirmations and intentions which I reference below have come from inspiring works of Dr. Wayne Dyer, Marianne Williamson, Iyanla Vanzant, Michael Bernard Beckwith and many others.

A. Meditation/breathing

Meditation is a practice to calm your mind, body and spirit. To become connected with your source, be present in the moment and focus on one thing. We can achieve this through traditional methods of meditation, sitting in peace and breathing or chanting, focusing on our source and divinity. Meditation can be practiced spiritually, but it can also be practiced in a secular manner by focusing on one task at a time, such as gardening, washing dishes or listening to music. Dr. Joan Borysenko reminds us that, through meditation,

> "In this state...intuition leads to deeper wisdom, the natural healing system of the body is engaged, our best physical and mental potential manifests itself, and we feel psychologically satisfied. Spiritual meditation will help you become aware of the presence of the divine in nature, in yourself and in other people. The love and joy that are inherent in Spirit—that is the very essence of Spirit—will begin to permeate your life."

Four things you can focus on when meditating:

1. You cannot know the meaning of your life until you are connected to the power that created you.

2. You are not this body, you are not this mind, and you are the spirit.

3. You have to know your spirit in order to know the truth.

4. Meditation is the only way you grow. It is how you make conscious contact with God.

B. Prayer/gratitude

Everyone has a different relationship with God. Some have no relationship, and that used to be me. At that point, I remember how uncomfortable I used to feel when people spoke about God or tried to proselytize me into a certain religion. So, for clarity here, I believe that prayer is for everyone. I believe in a God who is based in love and is within all of us. I pass no judgment on anyone's religious or spiritual beliefs, and I am accepting of whatever you believe. For me the transformation to believing in a power greater than myself has brought me great comfort, purpose and connection. I never feel alone. I now feel connected to a higher power and to everyone around me. It is a wonderful feeling.

For myself prayer starts with thanking God for all the things I am grateful for. I speak out loud everything I can think of: "Dear God, thank you for waking me up this morning. Thank you for protecting myself and my family. Thank you for our mental and physical health. Thank you for my loving husband and children. Thank you for my warm and nurturing home.

Thank you for the food in the refrigerator. Thank you for the money in my bank account to pay for all of my necessities." The list can go on and on. Think about everything that you are grateful for, and speak it into the world. This is a great way to start the day, because it brings focus to all of the blessings we have, and as we go throughout the day, they are always in the forefront of our mind. After giving thanks, I move on to asking for God to grant me certain things that I think will bring abundance into my life.

Sarah Ban Breathnach recites a prayer that I love to use daily in *Simple Abundance: A Daybook of Comfort and Joy*:

> Oh, God, give me grace for this day.
> Not for a lifetime, nor for the next week,
> Nor for tomorrow, just for this day.
> Direct my thoughts and bless them,
> Direct my work and bless it.
> Direct the things I say and give them blessings, too.
> Direct and bless everything that I think and speak and do.
> So that for this one day, just this one day,
> I have the gift of grace that comes from your presence...

Prayer helps me to feel united with God and everyone in the world for a greater purpose. This sense of connection brings me faith that everything will be fine no matter what happens, because I know we are all in this together. Rabbi Louis Bienstock explains in *The Power of Faith*,

> "Man was born together—all of one piece. It is the kind of world he has fashioned that has torn him apart. A world of folly! A world of falsehood! A world of fear! With the power of faith, let him

> put himself together again—faith in himself, faith in his fellowmen, faith in his destiny, faith in his God. Then and only then will man find happiness and peace."

Here are some other prayer statements that I have picked up along the way that resonate with me.

- Dear God, please give my life some sense of purpose, use me as an instrument of your peace, and use my talents and abilities to spread love.
- I surrender my job to you. Help me to remember that my real job is to love the world back to health.
- Dear God, I surrender the past to you.
- Please allow only loving, helpful thoughts about the past to remain in my mind and all the rest to be let go.
- Dear God, I surrender to you all of my thoughts about money.
- I surrender to you my debts; I surrender to you my wealth.
- Open my mind to receive abundantly.
- Channel your abundance through me in a way that serves the world.

C. Affirmations and intentions

Affirmations are positive, motivating statements. Intentions are statements regarding what you will do or want to do. Both affirmations and intentions are extremely powerful tools to align your thoughts and feelings with the dreams you have for your life. Write down your affirmations and intentions and record them. Each day, in the morning and at night, read them or listen to them to imprint your mind and the universe with your positive affirmations and your intentions for your life. In the morning when you wake and in the evening before you sleep are the most important times to practice this, because these are the times when our subconscious mind is the most receptive to reprogramming. Have you ever noticed that the first ten minutes when you wake up can set the tone for your entire day? We have a choice of how we are going to start our day; we can wake up and think, *I don't really want to get up, I am so tired. Oh, I can't stand my job, and I know it is going to be a bad day. I look terrible today. There is really no point in making an effort with my appearance. I can't wait for the day to be over so I can go back to sleep.* These thoughts create the intention for your day, and the universe does its job of bringing to you evidence to prove your intentions to be correct. So what happens? You go to work and you feel tired, you feel unattractive, and you gravitate negative interactions your direction at work. Well, there you go—you have just manifested your intention for that day!

In contrast, try waking up and saying, "Thank you, God, for this day! Please grant me a day's worth of grace. This is going to be a fantastic day. I feel strong, healthy and beautiful. I intend to bring peace and love to all those I touch. I look forward to the positive experiences the day will bring." What do you think happens? You put the message out there, and you begin to experience all that you intended. You wake up feeling great. You make connections with people in the coffee shop and bus stop on the way to work. You get to work with a smile and a positive attitude, and your coworkers and supervisor want to be around you. You begin to rub off on them, changing the work environment and the world for the better. It really is a simple practice, but many of us are unaware of the ways we stand in our own way.

Reading or listening to the affirmations and intentions at night before bed is especially effective, because you are feeding your subconscious mind with a ton of positive and abundant thoughts before bed. The subconscious mind works all night long, reprogramming your brain with these thoughts. Doing so opens the doors of your mind to allow the divine spirit to flow in and guide you. If there is a question you have or a problem you want to solve, speak it into the universe before bed, and you often will wake with the clarity to know which way to go. This is why it is so important not to take in negative images before bed through reading or watching television. Your subconscious mind will process those images and messages all night, trying to manifest them for you. Stay focused on what you want for your life and for our world, and feed your brain with those positive affirmations and intentions. You will be surprised how powerful this tool is.

Place copies of the affirmations and intentions around your home (on the bathroom mirror), in your car (on the dashboard) and at work (on your desk). Whenever you are feeling low or recognize defeating thoughts or statements, turn to these affirmations to change the script in your head and keep you moving in the right direction. Below I have listed many of the affirmation and intention statements I enjoy using, which I have accumulated from the various sources mentioned in this book, and primarily from Dr. Wayne Dyer's *The Power of Intention.*

- I choose happiness today. I choose success today. I choose right action today. I choose love and goodwill for all today. I choose peace today.
- I like money. I use it wisely, constructively and judiciously. I release it with joy and it returns to me thousand fold.
- By day and night, I am being prospered in all of my interests.

- I am relaxed and at peace, poised, balanced, serene and calm.
- I can do all things through the power of my subconscious mind.
- I have nothing to fear.
- Where there is sadness, let me bring joy. Where there is despair, let me bring hope. I am willing to let go of struggle and eager to learn through joy.
- I intend to take my mind off of problems and focus on what I want to manifest into my life.
- I can see beauty everywhere.
- I am whole and perfect as I was created.
- I attract only peace and peaceful people into my life. That is all I will allow.

D. Visualization

We have the ability to create the life of our dreams through many different interrelated techniques. One of these is visualization. The mind cannot tell the difference between an experience that you imagine with your vision and one that that you experience for real. When you show your mind an image either literally or mentally, it sets in motion the process of manifesting this experience for you. The tool of visualization is used widely and known to be very effective. Ivy Haley points out in *Discovering Your Purpose*,

> "Olympic athletes visualize themselves winning the race, scoring the touchdown or performing with skill and accuracy—before the competition begins. Professional speakers envision their audi-

> ences responding to a superb performance. Sales managers encourage staff members to imagine themselves making the sale before they meet with clients. Patients who visualize and think positively about their healing are more likely to mend rapidly and with less hardship."

You can visualize your goals by picturing them in your mind or creating a vision board. To do so, take as many pictures as possible that represent your authentic life full of passion, purpose and abundance. Get a bulletin board, and cut and paste these images to the board, sprinkling it with your arts-and-crafts creativity. This is a great activity to do with friends, family and even your children. It is never too early to learn the power of visualization in realizing your dreams!

Questions:

1. Which of these tools, if not all, will you begin to implement into your daily life?

____
____
____
____
____
____

2. What benefits will you experience from a greater connection to your source and to the universal community of all living things?

____
____
____
____
____
____

CONCLUSION

If there's anything I hope you will take away from reading this book, it is that you already "have it all" inside of you. Love yourself, put yourself first and follow your dreams. Step into your greatness and embrace your full power. Life will continue to send hurdles, but with heightened consciousness, you will leap over them with grace and beauty. As time goes on, there will be many more lessons to learn along the way, and so life continues...